# MEXICO MODERN

# MEXICO MODERN
## ARCHITECTURE AND INTERIORS

TAMI CHRISTIANSEN

PHOTOGRAPHY BY RICHARD POWERS

FOREWORD BY EUGENIO LÓPEZ ALONSO

New York · Paris · London · Milan

## Contents


| | | |
|---|---|---|
| | 12 | Foreword / Eugenio López Alonso |
| | 14 | Introduction |
| **Iconic** | 16 | PRAXIS / Agustín Hernández Navarro / Mexico City |
| | 28 | CASA JARDÍN ORTEGA / Luis Barragán / Mexico City |
| | 42 | PALACIO DE VERSALLES / Ricardo Legorreta / Mexico City |
| | 54 | CUADRA SAN CRISTÓBAL / Luis Barragán / Atizapán de Zaragoza |
| | 64 | CASA ORGÁNICA / Javier Senosiain / Naucalpan de Juárez |
| **Country** | 78 | CASA BERNAL / Chic by Accident / Bernal |
| | 92 | CASA COSECHA DE LLUVIA / JSa Arquitectura & Robert Hutchison Architecture / Temascaltepec |
| | 104 | CASA ALFEREZ / Ludwig Godefroy Architecture / Cañada de Alferes |
| | 114 | CASA DE TIERRA-CATARINA / Taller Héctor Barroso / Valle de Bravo |
| | 128 | CASA SANTA CATARINA / Emmanuel Picault / Morelos |
| | 138 | CASA IZAR / Taller ADG / Valle de Bravo |
| | 150 | LA COLINA FRENTE A LA CAÑADA / HW Studio Arquitectos / Morelia |
| **City** | 162 | CASA TEPETATE / Manuel Cervantes Studio / Mexico City |
| | 172 | CASA COYOACÁN / Pedro Reyes & Carla Fernández / Mexico City |
| | 190 | ESTUDIO GRACIELA ITURBIDE / Taller de Arquitectura Mauricio Rocha + Gabriela Carrillo / Mexico City |
| | 200 | CASA ESTUDIO / Manuel Cervantes Studio / Mexico City |
| | 210 | LA PLATANERA / Alberto Kalach / Mexico City |
| | 224 | CASA BO / IZ Arquitectos / Mexico City |
| | 234 | CASA MEZCAL / Barde vanVoltt / Mexico City |
| | 246 | CASA ESCUELA / Ezequiel Farca & Mónica Calderón / Mérida |
| **Beach** | 258 | CASA MONTE / Carlos H. Matos / Oaxaca |
| | 268 | CASA VIENTO / Aranza de Ariño / Oaxaca |
| | 278 | CASA NAILA / BAAQ / Oaxaca |
| | 288 | CASA ALTANERA / TAC / Oaxaca |
| | 298 | VILLA CAVA / Espacio 18 Arquitectura / Tulum |
| | 306 | CASA CONS / Bosco Sodi / Oaxaca |
| | 318 | CASA AVIV / CO-LAB Design Office / Tulum |
| | 326 | LA EXTRAVIADA / EM Estudio / Oaxaca |
| | 336 | CASA SHALVA / Arquitectura Mixta & Aviv Siso / Tulum |
| | 346 | Acknowledgments |

# Foreword

**Eugenio López Alonso**

I am proud to present this carefully curated selection of the most significant architectural works of iconic and contemporary Mexican architecture, which has proved to be a powerful expression of cultural identity, innovation, and profound respect for the natural environment. These works have arisen from the combination of ancestral traditions with a modern vision; Mexican architectural practices have found inspiration in the country's diverse and rich geography, the warmth of its light, and the need to create sustainable spaces that are in harmony with their surroundings.

It is important to highlight the organic and constant dialogue between nature and architecture. Rather than imposing their work on the landscape, these architects seek to integrate it with its surroundings through the use of native materials such as adobe, tepetate, volcanic rock, tezontle, cantera stone, clay, and local woods that not only reduce the climate footprint but also evoke a sense of belonging and continuity with the past. By designing spaces that respect topography, vegetation, and ecosystems, they generate architecture that feels alive, harmonious, and deeply rooted.

The use of light as a vital element in the design of a building is also worth emphasizing: light is treated as an additional material; patios, lattices, and skylights transform interior spaces during the day through the changing color of the light, creating sensorial spaces in constant transition.

Finally, I invite the reader to explore Mexico with fresh eyes and discover in every wall, shadow, material, and texture a story that connects the present, past, and future.

## Introduction

*Mexico Modern* is a rich portfolio of modern Mexican architecture and design crafted by some of the country's most innovative architects, designers, and artists. It is a visual diary that explores the architectural diversity of Mexico, presenting homes that offer a profound sense of place through the lens of exceptional design.

The opening section focuses on four revered iconic Mexican architects—Agustín Hernández Navarro, Luis Barragán, Ricardo Legorreta, and Javier Senosiain—whose enduring legacies and legendary works continue to influence modern architecture and shape international architectural discourse. This sets the stage for a showcase of extraordinary homes across varied topographies, designed by the nation's leading modern architects and designers. These profiles include both established and emerging talents who are recognized for their adventurous and innovative approaches to design. Pushing the boundaries of convention and creating spaces that transcend mere functionality to become true works of art, this work is characterized by architectural experimentation and creativity, marking these mavericks as future icons.

More than a book, *Mexico Modern* is a compendium, a celebration of exceptional homes, set against the stunning backdrop of regional landscapes, and the creative talents behind them. It invites readers to explore important cultural sites where architecture is deeply influenced by its location and history. The book documents a curated selection of dwellings—from natural homes that blend seamlessly into rural settings to bold urban structures that manipulate form and space, to sculptural seaside sanctuaries that stand as temples in the sand. Through these pages, doors are opened to architectural feats, each capturing a distinctive essence of this vibrant and diverse country, paying homage to the country's rich heritage, its building traditions, and its skilled artisans.

## Praxis / Agustín Hernández Navarro

Agustín Hernández Navarro (1924–2022), an iconic figure in Mexican modernism, embraced a fusion of sculpture and architecture in his designs. Among his notable creations, Praxis (1975) stands out as the quintessential example. This brutalist home / studio is dramatically cantilevered, appearing to levitate over the Bosques de las Lomas neighborhood in Mexico City. Designed as his personal retreat, the structure allowed Hernández Navarro to sequester himself away from the urban sprawl and provided a unique space to foster his creative pursuits.

The building, inspired by the concept of a tree house, integrates geometric forms with organic motifs. Constructed from prisms and pyramids, the structure rises over 130 feet, asserting a monumental presence amidst the foliage. Despite its robust concrete composition and sharp angles, there is an inherent lightness to its verticality, reminiscent of a tree trunk. The foundation, secured by deep-set steel rods, mirrors the natural mechanics of a tree and its roots, ensuring stability through a combination of tension and compression.

Central to Hernández Navarro's approach was the design of the vertical elements. A spiral staircase with triangular metal steps forms the core of the building. This feature is not only functional but also serves as a sculptural element, further emphasized by a large spherical window that frames the verdant canopy outside. These design elements—circles, triangles, squares, and rectangles—are recurrent throughout Hernández Navarro's work, reflecting his deep commitment to geometric principles. He famously stated, "Geometry is my religion," underscoring his belief in the fundamental role of shapes in expressing universal truths about time, space, and dualities inherent in nature and human culture.

Hernández Navarro's architectural philosophy was deeply influenced by ancient Mesoamerican aesthetics combined with Le Corbusier-inspired forms. His buildings are characterized by their monolithic structures, reaching towards the sky while remaining grounded in their cultural heritage. He skillfully incorporated elements of Mexico's pre-Columbian past into his architecture, achieving a synthesis of form, function, and historical narrative. Hernández Navarro insisted that architectural design must adhere to functionality, rejecting arbitrary forms in favor of those steeped in mathematical and rhythmic precision.

Hernández Navarro notably chose to eschew color in his architectural designs, contrasting sharply with such contemporaries as Luis Barragán and Ricardo Legorreta. He argued that form alone should define space, and he used light and shadow to accentuate materials without the need for color, which he likened to superficial makeup.

Over his lifetime, Hernández Navarro contributed a remarkable range of projects, from the Heroico Colegio Militar, also in Mexico City, to various residential and cultural buildings, each marked by a forward-thinking, innovative approach. His most significant works, like the Meditation Center and the Folkloric Ballet School in Cuernavaca, showcase a blend of futuristic, organic, and brutalist elements, all hallmarks of his unique style.

Agustín Hernández Navarro was a visionary whose legacy bridges the expansive ideals of mid-century urban planning and modern architectural innovations. His commitment to exploring new forms and solutions left an indelible mark on Mexican architecture, ensuring his place as a pivotal figure in the narrative of twentieth-century modernism. His diverse and paradoxical body of work continues to inspire and challenge the norms of architectural design, making every structure a distinct expression of his philosophical and aesthetic convictions.

Kahn
MEXICO
HI-TEC ARCHITECTURE
HISTORIA DE LA ARQUITECTURA Y EL URBANISMO MEXICANOS
www.trespa.com

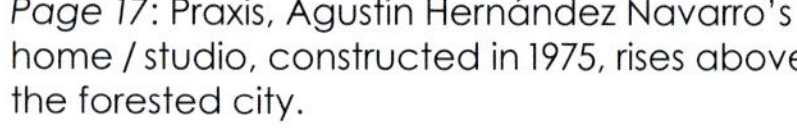

*Page 17*: Praxis, Agustín Hernández Navarro's home / studio, constructed in 1975, rises above the forested city.

*Preceding pages, left*: Built from a set of prisms and pyramids, the residence's sculptural geometric forms and bold proportions reflect the architect's visionary approach.

*Preceding pages, right*: Preserved as a time capsule, the top-floor library houses the architect's books, objects, and furnishings.

*Right*: Panoramic city and forest vistas are on full display from the living room, which features original furnishings. Suspended in a concrete tree, Hernández Navarro was able to work, visualize, and disconnect from the world in his home / studio.

*Right*: The bedroom's built-in furnishings, splayed walls, and glazed and carpeted surfaces soften the interiors, and contrast with the building's austere exterior.

*Following pages, left*: Circulation defines the design. Stairs link the entry to the workspace and private quarters above.

*Following pages, right*: Metal spiral stairs—tensioned by springs and supports—serve both structural and sculptural roles. A large spherical window frames the forest canopy.

*Right*: Though monumental, Hernández Navarro's work conveys a sense of lightness—the geometric concrete form appears to soar, defying gravity.

## Casa Jardín Ortega / Luis Barragán

Ortega Garden House, one of the lesser-known and enigmatic projects by Luis Barragán (1902–1988), exudes simplicity, austerity, and an intriguing sense of mystery. As the foundational project in Barragán's career, it set the stage for his later, more well-known works.

Barragán, Mexico's most celebrated architect, is renowned for his invaluable contribution to architecture. His designs, firmly rooted in harmonious and poetic principles, reflect a deeply personal quest for beauty and serenity—a journey celebrated by the Pritzker Prize Jury in 1980 when they honored him with architecture's highest award.

Barragán's work is marked by a stoic acceptance of solitude, which he believed to be intrinsic to the human experience, and in his acceptance speech, he spoke of the essential elements of beauty, silence, solitude, serenity, death, and happiness. The master envisioned his buildings as sanctuaries where one could reconcile with oneself amid the vastness of life and the inevitability of death.

Situated in Tacubaya, Mexico City, the Ortega Garden House was the first house Barragán designed and inhabited. Completed in 1942, it marks a pivotal moment in his career. Living there until 1947, he infused the home with rich details, colors, and atmospheric qualities that make it a national treasure. Today, the house remains unchanged, preserving not only the architectural elements but also the original gardens, spatial sequences, and furnishings from that era.

From the outside, the building presents a facade of modesty and restraint, suggesting the wealth of character hidden within. Now listed by UNESCO on its World Heritage List, the home invites visitors into its embrace with iconic pink walls—a Barragán signature—leading to an interior rich with textiles, art, and original furniture by such designers as Clara Porset, Michael van Beuren, and Barragán himself.

This garden house, along with the museum house next-door—also designed and inhabited by Barragán—represents a unique exploration of vernacular and colonial themes. Yet it is not merely a replication of those styles but a reimagining that incorporates modern architectural sensibilities.

Inside, the garden remains a hidden sanctuary, a lush, opulent retreat that reveals itself only upon entering the home. Inspired by the Alhambra's patios and gardens, Barragán's design includes meandering paths, stone sculptures, and tranquil water features. He once described his vision for the garden as an attempt to "create a garden in compartments," reminiscent of majestic Spanish landscapes.

The gardens, together with the faded-rose-colored walls, bearing the marks of time, evoke the soft glow of sunset, reflecting Barragán's mastery in capturing and manipulating light. The current owner, a descendant of the Ortega family who acquired the home from Barragán in 1947, verifies that the walls were first left white, serving as a blank canvas, but later adorned with colors reflecting the surrounding natural light.

More than eighty years later, the gardens have been meticulously preserved, maintaining their design integrity and natural beauty despite the urban sprawl encroaching upon them. These gardens not only showcase Barragán's skill as an architect but also his visionary landscape design, which remains relevant and influential.

Today, Casa Ortega and its gardens are as Luis Barragán envisioned them—a reflection of the memories from his childhood haciendas colored by the garden designs of Ferdinand Bac and Barragán's encounters with modern European architecture. They embody his lifelong inspirations: beauty, magic, enchantment, serenity, silence, intimacy, and amazement. These principles guided his architectural endeavors, leaving a lasting legacy that continues to inspire and captivate.

*Page 29*: Ortega Garden House is the first residence designed and inhabited by Luis Barragán. Locatod in Tacubaya, Moxico City, it represents the foundation of his architectural language.

*Preceding pages, left*: The entry hall features Barragán's bold use of color, establishing a sense of harmony, and offers a subtle reveal of the interior spaces beyond.

*Preceding pages, right*: Completed in 1942, the house exemplifies early expressions of Barragán's signature spatial and chromatic sensibilities. The living and dining areas are furnished with original mid-century pieces by Clara Porset, Michael van Beuren, George Nelson, and Barragán himself, in collaboration with his cabinetmaker Eleuterio Cortés.

*Opposite*: View to the garden sanctuary glimpsed through the large window in the dining area.

*Following pages, left*: A corridor highlights Barragan's refined detailing—simple, yet expressive of his architectural ethos.

*Following pages, right*: The home studio features Barragán's drawing table and furnishings. Amber glass bottles and perforated shutters introduce warmth and material richness.

*Left*: The terrace, furnished with a rustic wooden table, benches, and chairs, reflects Barragán's integration of landscape and architecture, creating a cohesive outdoor environment.

*Following pages, left*: Foliage spills onto the patio, becoming an integral part of the structure.

*Following pages, right*: Sculptures are placed throughout the gardens. Here, a female form rests amid lush greenery.

*Page 40*: Inspired by the patios and gardens of the Alhambra, Barragán's design incorporates meandering paths, stone sculptures, and tranquil water features, inviting quiet reflection.

*Page 41*: Meticulously preserved, the gardens retain their natural beauty and exemplify Barragán's poetic approach to landscape design—one that remains both relevant and influential today.

## Palacio de Versalles / Ricardo Legorreta

Palacio de Versalles is the iconic residence of the prolific Ricardo Legorreta (1931–2011), who designed and built the modernist home for his family in 1957 as a canvas for his pioneering vision.

Located in Mexico City's Lomas de Reforma neighborhood, the residence, set on a steep slope, offers encompassing views of the adjacent canyon. This challenging site spurred Legorreta to find ingenious architectural solutions, prioritizing privacy and the integration of the natural landscape into the living experience. The home's layout descends along the hillside; private living spaces are nestled below, with only the garage and service areas accessible from street level. This arrangement fosters seclusion and facilitates a direct connection with the outdoor environment, elements central to Legorreta's design philosophy.

Trained under Luis Barrágan, Legorreta was deeply influenced by his mentor's ethos, but quickly charted his own path. Palacio de Versalles showcases this distinctive style, characterized by robust protective walls, hidden courtyards, and a vibrant interplay of colors against clean lines and geometric simplicity.

Legorreta's architectural approach reflects a departure from conventional modernism. He often eschewed the use of glass curtain walls, favoring instead the solidity of thick walls and the intimacy of hidden courtyards. Emphasis is given to walls—as screens, ornaments, gateways, backgrounds for murals—to delineate spaces and separate functions, and to ensure privacy and provoke a sense of mystery. His designs engage the senses, creating a procession of spaces that play with light and shadow to produce dramatic, almost theatrical effects. Details such as grid-patterned windows and strategically placed bursts of color enhance these dynamic interactions, adding layers of depth and intrigue to his structures.

Throughout his extensive career, his bold use of color, dramatic spatial arrangements, and incorporation of traditional Mexican elements garnered international acclaim, attracting clients worldwide. Rugged textures, unusual angling, and unexpected glints of color give his structures their evocative, emotional appeal. Legoretta's diverse design portfolio—whose projects are concerned with light, color, walls, courtyards, scale, water, humor, and social conscience—includes everything from residential homes to major commercial projects, each stamped with his unique architectural signature.

Today, Ricardo Legorreta's son upholds his legacy at Studio Legorreta, which Legorreta established in 1965. The firm continues from its offices adjacent to Palacio de Versalles, where the studio remains committed to a design philosophy rooted in humanistic values, striving to create spaces that promote privacy, peace, and optimism. Through their ongoing work, the enduring principles of Legorreta's architecture continue to influence and inspire, securing his place as a pillar of global architectural heritage.

*Page 43*: Grid-patterned windows and vibrant color accents create layered spatial experiences—hallmarks of Legorreta's architectural narrative.

*Pages 44–45*: The entry stairs to Palacio de Versalles. Ricardo Legorreta designed this modernist home for his family in 1957 as a personal canvas for his visionary architectural ideals. He became known for reinterpreting traditional Mexican architecture through bold colors, geometric forms, and intimate, light-filled spaces.

*Preceding pages*: Legorreta's design presents a sense of enclosure and protection, provided by thick walls and hidden courtyards.

*Opposite*: Legorreta often designed furniture tailored to each project. Shown here is the dining room with his Vallarta pine table and woven palm chairs—modern takes on traditional Mexican forms. Produced by Legorreta Arquitectos in 1972, the Vallarta Collection was originally created for Camino Real hotels in Ixtapa, Cancún, and Puerto Vallarta.

*Following pages, left*: Legorreta's work always responded to place and people. Shown here is a custom-designed kitchen.

*Following pages, right*: Bold color juxtaposed with curved lines and spare geometric forms make up this staircase.

*Page 52*: Influenced by Mexican heritage, and colonial history and architecture, Legorreta often incorporated courtyards and vivid palettes into his work.

*Page 53*. The terrace of the residence, in the Lomas de Reforma neighborhood, is situated on a steep slope to capture sweeping canyon and city views. The round table, also by Legorreta, exemplifies his use of natural materials and the seamless integration of furniture with architecture.

## Cuadra San Cristóbal / Luis Barragán

A masterpiece of scale and sequencing designed by Luis Barragán, Cuadra San Cristóbal stands as a powerful display of geometric precision and a profound appreciation for simplicity. Completed in 1968 in the district of Los Clubes, this modernist ranch was commissioned by the Egerstrom family, who continue to reside there. The estate is heralded as one of Barragán's most iconic works, instantly recognizable by its pink and mauve walls, a striking azure fountain, and its bold, geometric forms. It encompasses a residence, horse stables, and auxiliary facilities, cleverly integrating living and equestrian spaces.

The design of Cuadra San Cristóbal, influenced by Barragán's passion for equestrian culture, features the interplay of minimalist elements with dramatic bursts of color—a hallmark of his architecture. A prominent pink stucco wall creates a north-south division across the property, separating it into two distinct areas. The western section is narrower, while the larger eastern area houses the private quarters of the estate. This wall is punctuated by two large rectangular openings tall enough to accommodate horses and riders, linking the separate zones both visually and physically.

At the center of the estate, a gradually sloping basin, initially intended to be filled via an aqueduct, now features a grand fountain fed by a source in the monumental wall. Barragán's design provides continuity through the use of water, adding elements of dynamic movement and tranquility while integrating the architectural forms; the landscape not only complements the architecture, but rather becomes it.

Barragán's design philosophy embraces fluidity where geometric lines are not confined to rigidity. Instead, they are enhanced by imaginative uses of color and texture, engaging the natural elements of water and earth to create a sensory experience. This approach is not just functional but deeply poetic, reflecting Barragán's belief in the emotive power of architecture.

When Barragán's contributions to architecture were honored with the Pritzker Prize in 1980, the jury praised him for treating architecture as a "sublime act of the poetic imagination," creating spaces of "haunting beauty" that serve as metaphysical landscapes for meditation and companionship. His work at Cuadra San Cristóbal epitomizes this philosophy, melding artistic vision with practical design to forge an environment of serene beauty and functionality.

Today, Cuadra San Cristóbal is a significant landmark in the narrative of Mexican modernism. Its blend of tranquil azure waters, vibrant pink walls, and touches of crisp white and russet stand as testaments to Barragán's signature style. As one of the most influential Mexican architects of the twentieth century, Barragán professed, "Architecture is an art when one consciously or unconsciously creates aesthetic emotion in the atmosphere and when this environment produces well-being."

The iconic master clearly understood the spiritual value of architecture. Through Cuadra San Cristóbal, Luis Barragán's architectural legacy continues to inspire and resonate, transcending the ordinary, inviting all who visit to experience the profound impact of thoughtfully-designed architecture and built environments.

*Page 55*: One of Luis Barragán's most iconic works, Cuadra San Cristóbal is a private estate comprising a residence, horse stables, and auxiliary facilities—an enduring example of his masterful integration of architecture, landscape, and color.

*Preceding pages*: Cuadra San Cristóbal stands as a significant legacy of Mexican modernism. Its tranquil fountains and serene azure tones are set against deep russet and vivid pink walls—colors that have come to symbolize Barragán's distinctive work, recognized worldwide.

*Opposite*: The use of water is a masterful way to convey a sense of calm while adding movement and energy to the estate.

*Following pages*: The compound's striking pink walls, russet accents, and water feature are testimony to Barragán's unique design philosophy.

*Pages 62–63*: An equestrian enthusiast, Barragán developed the estate in collaboration with his colleague and equestrian friend Andrés Casillas. The property is enjoyed by all creatures great and small.

*Preceding page*: Iconic Mexican architect Javier Senosiain, known for his organic, fantastical designs, created this family home on a hillside outside Mexico City in 1984. The architect decided to add a fin to the residence after its construction workers started calling it "The Shark."

*Opposite*: This semi-buried home blends into the landscape, wrapped in a green ridge that renders it nearly invisible. The living room's curved window and eave, resembling an eye with lashes, shields the space from the elements. According to Senosiain, organic architecture seeks harmony between people and nature.

*Following pages*: Sparsely furnished, the living room and kitchen were designed with intention. In the living room, a built-in curved leather sofa bench follows the window's arc, framing views of nature. Key pieces include a hanging rattan swing seat and an original Hand Chair by Mexican artist Pedro Friedeberg. Set against the natural backdrop of the sand-toned interiors, minimal organic shelving with rounded edges and the smooth contours of the counter are distinct features in the kitchen.

*Page 70*: In the bedroom, integrated furnishings enhance spatial flow. A sculptural handbasin and counters reflect the home's fluid aesthetic.

*Page 71*: A cocoon-like seating niche is carved into the entry tunnel hall, offering a moment of stillness upon arrival.

*Preceding pages*: A tunnel leads to the primary suite—designed for rest and function. Built-in niches and a custom bed that doubles as a daybed echo the room's curvature, underscoring the organic design. The earth-toned walls and ceiling unify the space chromatically with the carpeted floor in a sandy hue evoking the feeling of dwelling within the earth itself.

*Left*: Carved niches and round-edged shelving provide functional storage for clothing while maintaining the natural flow of the dressing room and bathroom, shown beyond, with its molded handbasin and wooden cabinet detailing.

*Following pages, left*: In the children's room, sleeping alcoves with built in beds and shelving offer only the essentials—each detail carefully considered by the architect.

*Following pages, right*: Sculptural elements and sinuous forms echo nature and the organic narrative.

A distinctive project by the architecture and design studio Chic by Accident, Casa Bernal rises from the foundational ruins of a sixteenth-century colonial mansion in the state of Querétaro, Central Mexico. This masterful architectural endeavor is strategically positioned within view of the Peña de Bernal, a monolithic guardian and UNESCO-listed natural monument.

Casa Bernal's design engages in a profound dialogue with the monolith, an eight-million-year-old sentinel that towers over the landscape. According to architect Emmanuel Picault, the monumental concrete structure reveres and responds to its colossal neighbor. It is positioned both as an observer and a participant within this geological theater, establishing a connection that is both aesthetic and spiritual, transforming the site into a contemporary temple where nature and architecture convene together.

The site's challenging terrain, with its steep, rocky topography, required innovative architectural solutions. The layout and material choices, including the use of concrete and volcanic stone, were informed by Picault's weekly observations of the site's changing light and shadows, ensuring that the house addresses its physical context as well as considering the cultural and spiritual significance of the monolith.

The architect's design philosophy extends beyond mere construction; it supports acts of narrative creation. Picault's design of Casa Bernal is a masterful orchestration of forms and materials, revering the landscape. It acts as a sanctuary, subtly engaging with the dramatic vistas and historical echoes of its location. The integration of the ruins of the mansion which previously occupied the site, adorned with cacti and desert flora, serves as a tangible link to the past. These remnants, coupled with the new structures, create a dialogue between time periods, each enhancing the other's aesthetic and structural narrative, allowing the past and present to coexist.

Picault's design emphasizes fluidity and integration between indoor and outdoor environments. The house features living spaces arranged around external features—terraces, patios, and a central pool—which serve as the "lungs" in an arid landscape. This integration extends to the use of materials, blending the ruggedness of stone with the smoothness of concrete, and linking the arid exterior with the home's serene interiors.

Inside, architectural elements are designed to capture natural light and frame views of the monolith, with tall, narrow windows and doors strategically placed to enhance perspective. The interior space is defined by minimalism and functionality, with a gallery-like ambiance that is both serene and livable. Furnishings, often built into the structure itself, include pieces made of concrete and tropical wood, complemented by curated pieces from Chic by Accident Atelier. This selection celebrates the legacy of Mexico's mid-century designers while also drawing inspiration from the geometric and symbolic richness of ancient cultures that resonate with Picault's designs.

Emmanuel Picault's work is deeply influenced by the shapes, symbols, and spirit of pre-Hispanic culture. His designs, much like poetry, are born from a profound emotional response to the surroundings, crafting spaces that are both a sanctuary and a spectacle, inviting those who enter to experience the blending of past and present in ways that are both grand and intimate.

Casa Bernal stands as a poetic composition in concrete and stone, a place of living heritage and modern innovation where every design element is a stanza in a longer poem of place, culture, history, and creativity.

*Page 79*: Carved into the rocky slopes of Peña de Bernal in Querétaro, three hours from Mexico City, Casa Bernal by Emmanuel Picault of Chic by Accident is a home that merges with the landscape in a singularly sculptural way.

*Pages 80–81*: Engaging in a silent dialogue with the sacred mountain, the house serves as both witness and participant. "Like a temple, it faces its deity," Picault reflects. "It looks, worships, contemplates—and turns its back to feel its own strength." Cacti stand as sentinels around the pool, their deep blue-green hue shifting with the arc of the sun.

*Pages 82–83*: The interior is a study in restraint. A gallery-like atmosphere lets form and light speak. Centered in the dining space are the Vallarta table and woven chairs by Ricardo Legorreta framed by soaring vertical windows with a view of the monolith. A trio of volcanic stone spheres by Chic by Accident Atelier grounds the space with bold contemporary artwork by Florian and Michael Quistrebert.

*Page 84*: Rounded forms echo the home's geometry. A sculpted concrete handbasin and shower—both designed by Chic by Accident—pay respect to the ritual of bathing.

*Page 85*: Defined by minimalism and functionality, the brutalist concrete kitchen's pared-back cylindrical shelving holds terra-cotta pottery crafted by local artisans. The structure stands as a sculpture.

*Page 86*: Accessed from a private courtyard, the primary bedroom is seen through tall glass doors, custom-crafted by a local blacksmith.

*Page 87*: The cylindrical shower and handcrafted copper tub reflect the home's sculptural intent. "I wanted something circular that created a sense of intimacy—and the acoustics make even a whistle sound beautiful," Picault notes.

*Preceding pages*: Time lingers in the layers of the old hacienda's facade, its patina left untouched. In the courtyard garden, tall iron and glass doors give way to a quiet dialogue between past and present.

*Left*: The living room within the original sixteenth-century mansion remains largely as it was—walls preserved, history intact. Custom concrete seating and monumental windows are the only modern updates. "I refused to touch the patina," Picault says. "It was about honoring what was already there."

## Casa Cosecha de Lluvia / JSA Arquitectura & Robert Hutchison Architecture

Situated in the mountainous region west of Mexico City, Rain Harvest Home, or Casa Cosecha de Lluvia, is a modest yet pioneering residence co-designed by Javier Sanchez Arquitectura (JSa) and Robert Hutchison Architecture. This tripartite wooden home, designed as a weekend retreat for Sanchez's family, is distinguished by its minimal impact on the environment, fulfilling a vision to live closely connected with nature by blending into the landscape and responding adaptively to its natural cycles. The goal was to take an integrated approach to building and living with nature and for the structures to make as little disturbance to the site as possible, accepting nature as a theater where architecture plays a supporting role.

Offering an experiential connection to place, the architectural configuration challenges traditional residential layouts by distributing the living spaces across three distinct wooden structures, each designed to be permeable and integrate with the surrounding terrain. The main cabin is the core of the residence, featuring essential living spaces. Complementing this are a bathhouse—equipped with a sauna, steam shower, and a central cold plunge pool open to the skies—and a separate bedroom studio that offers additional living and creative spaces, crowned with an upstairs patio. These structures are not just functional but are strategic in promoting an intimate interaction between the building's inhabitants and the environment.

A notable aspect of the design is its water autonomy. Each building is designed to collect rainwater, which is then filtered and stored on-site, providing a year-round water supply and making the home entirely self-sufficient in its water usage. This system is particularly significant here in Valle de Bravo, near Temascaltepec, a region named after pre-Hispanic sweat lodges, indicating a historical connection to innovative water use.

The home is part of a larger 450-acre development, La Reserva el Peñón, aimed at fostering a community that lives in balance with its surroundings. The development is built on principles of regenerative design, with every household required to capture a significant portion of their water needs from rainfall.

The community's broader water strategy includes an extensive network of reservoirs and bioswales, ensuring sustainability and resilience against environmental threats such as illegal logging and groundwater contamination. These choices were driven by the urgent need to address the local water shortage issues holistically, and to point out the paradox of the region's high rainfall, yet scarcity of available water.

Environmental considerations extend beyond hydrological strategies. The home and the larger reserve actively engage in soil regeneration through permaculture practices and a bio-agricuture garden that produces a substantial percentage of the family's food. This approach not only mitigates the impacts of dryness and erosion but also supports a richer biodiversity within the conserved area, which makes up most of the reserve.

The selection of materials further reflects the project's environmental philosophy. By opting for wood over traditional masonry or concrete, the design reduces the carbon footprint and supports long-term sustainability.

More than a place of dwelling, it is a demonstrative project that invites its occupants and the wider community to rethink how modern living can coexist with environmental stewardship. As the project evolves, it serves as a living laboratory for sustainable practices, continually adapting and learning from the natural world it seeks to protect. Through thoughtful design and innovative water management strategies, Casa Cosecha de Lluvia offers an example of what is possible when architecture and ecology converge.

*Page 93*: Located in the forested mountains of Temascaltepec, Rain Harvest Home integrates sustainability with design. Three distinct structures—a guest studio, bathhouse, and main residence—are connected by winding paths through native vegetation. A harvesting rainwater pond mirrors the sky and trees, reinforcing the home's integration with nature and connection to water.

*Page 94*: The bathhouse harvests rainwater, year-round, with a skylit cold-water plunge pool at its center. Encircling spaces include a tub, sauna, and steam shower—integrating design into the cycle of water and of life.

*Page 95*: Clad in charred timber, the interiors resonate with the rugged terrain. The living room, enveloped in blackened wood and softened with pale timber and volcanic stone, opens onto a garden patio. Furniture by Mexican designers Héctor Esrawe and Laura Natividad complements the space.

*Preceding pages*: A favorite gathering space, the outdoor living area centers around an open fireplace framed by a steel wall, with views into the kitchen. "We spend evenings here with friends, under the stars," shares architect Javier Sanchez.

*Opposite*: Vintage furnishings meet industrial finishes in the kitchen, where open stainless-steel shelves display handcrafted Mexican pottery. Recinto stone floors and black timber walls are a recurring feature throughout the residence.

*Following pages*: A wraparound porch offers dining with expansive views of the pond and misty morning landscape. Donald Judd–inspired furniture and Oaxacan ceramics celebrate craftsmanship and tradition.

*Page 102*: Rain Harvest Home is nestled in a forested region near Valle de Bravo. Set on a relatively flat plateau within the mountainous landscape, the home is surrounded by dense vegetation.

*Page 103*: Forested mountains frame the view through a large window in the double-height timber guest studio, which houses a bedroom, a bathroom, and an upper-level patio that opens to the landscape.

## Casa Alferez / Ludwig Godefroy Architecture

Designed by visionary architect Ludwig Godefroy, this cabin is an example of his innovative spirit and his unwavering commitment to pushing the boundaries of design. From its solid concrete exterior to its interior bathed in light, Casa Alferez is a demonstration of Godefroy's mastery of form and space.

Resting on a green slope in a pine forest on the outskirts of Mexico City, a deconstructed building hides among tall trees. Conceived as a "living sculpture," this unexpected neo-brutalist vault-like shelter, designed as a "nest" to generate feelings of safety, security, and peacefulness, feels serene and tranquil in the mountain landscape.

Resembling a fortress, this refuge seems comfortable in its natural surroundings. The geometries of its angular shell are punctuated by irregular windows that frame the surrounding landscape.

Referencing the morphology of the bunkers built during the Second World War in the architect's native Normandy as well as pre-Hispanic temples, Godefroy blends these influences, making them a distinctive feature and reoccuring motifs of his design language. The choice of simple, almost primitive materials—concrete for the structure, internal partitions, stairs, and platform overlooking the forest, and pinewood for the coverings and fixed furnishings—creates a fascinating visual dialogue.

Casa Alferez attests to Godefroy's mastery of space using form, material, and light. The house is defined by its verticality, reminiscent of a cathedral's proportions; curvilinear skylights and windows set high integrate soft, sculptural light, lending an almost transcendent, solemn, monastic poetry to the space. The architect describes his design process as akin to analog photography, playing with natural light to shape the interior environment, drawing parallels between the gradual development of a photograph and the design of a space.

After graduating from the École d'architecture de la ville et des territoires à Marne-la-Vallée in Paris, and working in the studios of Enric Miralles-Benedetta Tagliabue in Barcelona, OMA in Rotterdam, and Tatiana Bilbao in Mexico City, Godefroy chose Mexico City to found his design studio. "I'm not sure how I got here, but the only thing I know is why I didn't leave Mexico: simply because I have developed a tender and affectionate bond with this country," explains the designer, who gives great importance—in life as in his work—to the word "concordance." Godefroy explains, "It can be difficult to define: it can mean a similarity, a correspondence, a resonance, or a relationship. It is an extraordinary meeting point between things, a source of surprise, and for me, very often, a starting point for a project." In this case, it is about harmony with the place, which is treated by Godefroy with absolute respect, but also harmony with the client, a young professional from Mexico City.

At the center of the house, a series of stacked platforms and half levels create a sense of spatial depth, while an impressive concrete staircase serves as the centerpiece of the interior. An internal balcony on the landing between the office and the rooftop terrace creates space to reflect and view the voluminous sanctuary, measuring over twenty-one feet at its pinnacle. From the highest level, one can admire the complexity of the internal environments—stairs with sculptural geometries and double-height spaces intended for relaxation, conviviality, and private moments—arranged on several floors and visually connected to each other.

The custom-designed furnishings see an introduction of warm shades of wood in contrast with the rougher textures of the concrete perimeter walls. The focal element of the composition is the central deep-seated forest-green velvet sofa, designed as a square conversation pit, with rounded corners carved into the floor. This sort of enveloping nest was desired by the homeowner and the designer to emphasize the sense of welcome and casual hospitiality.

Godefroy's Casa Alferez surpasses its function as a shelter, asserting itself as a living sculpture. The home not only reflects Godefroy's architectural acumen but also his intuitive grasp of how spaces can evoke emotional responses, leaving a memorable impact on all who visit.

*Opposite*: From the dining area, located on a higher level, the complexity of the interior space is apparent. Concrete partitions and slabs define staggered floors dedicated to domestic functions, and platforms and mezzanines create vertical flow. A central sculptural concrete stairwell anchors the composition. From the highest level, a landing between the upper living space and the rooftop terrace invites moments of pause into the circulation with views of the lofty interior.

*Following pages*: A sanctuary in the mountains, conceived as a protective nest, the home offers a sense of retreat and stillness. The minimalist palette is softened through timber elements and custom furnishings that emphasize coherence. Artisan-made Mexican textiles add tactile contrast to the raw concrete envelope.

*Page 112*: The neo-brutalist villa is characterized by windows placed to frame glimpses of the landscape.

*Page 113*: In the kitchen, minimalist concrete surfaces and open shelving support material clarity and visual continuity within the larger space. A window frames the forest—reinforcing the architecture's ongoing dialogue with its natural surroundings. Angular walls and concrete surfaces are softened with the introduction of wooden flooring.

ANDO

## Casa de Tierra-Catarina / Taller Héctor Barroso

Conceived by Mexico City-based Taller Héctor Barroso, Casa de Tierra-Catarina appears as a serene enclave harmonizing with its picturesque lakeside environment in Valle de Bravo. This architectural endeavor utilizes rammed earth crafted into a series of six clay structures that echo the rugged red terrain and lush surroundings. With a deliberate "V" configuration, the layout enhances the dwelling's engagement with the vast landscape, offering sweeping views of both the adjacent lake and the imposing mountain backdrop.

The house gracefully transitions from communal to private areas, creating a flow that subtly blurs the boundaries between the built environment and the natural landscape. The strategic placement of these buildings allows for a rhythmic dance of opening and closing spaces, which not only ensures privacy, but also frames the majestic rock formations and verdant forest. The design philosophy here is one of subtle integration, with the rammed earth structures complementing the natural hues of the terrain, aspiring to be both unobtrusive and at one with the land.

Sustainability stands at the forefront of Casa de Tierra-Catarina's design ethos. The materials, all locally sourced, include clay-rich earth excavated from the site; this ecological approach extends to the home's functionality, where cross-ventilation and rainwater harvesting, employed to minimize the ecological footprint, help to maintain a comfortable living space.

The interiors, curated by Habitación 116, speak to a minimalist aesthetic that reflects the home's natural setting. This multidisciplinary design studio emphasizes a deep connection to Mexican cultural heritage, reinterpreting traditional customs and crafts to maintain a distinct national identity within a contemporary framework. The interior spaces employ a palette of understated tones and materials that reflect the landscape, reinforcing the home's seamless indoor / outdoor synergy.

Barroso, in collaboration with landscape architect Hugo Sanchez, articulates a vision where architecture and environment are in constant conversation. This philosophy manifests in a meticulous balance between manipulation and respect for the original site, striving for designs that go beyond temporal and stylistic confines. Barroso's architectural narrative is not limited to local attitudes; rather, it draws from a deeper regional context, aiming to create spaces that are both elemental and enduring.

Casa de Tierra-Catarina is a representation of modern Mexican architecture, where traditional techniques and local materials blend to form a setting that is both innovative and intimately tied to its cultural and environmental context. This project not only underscores the importance of architectural humility while preserving the integrity of the surrounding landscape, but also showcases how modern design can encapsulate timeless beauty and functionality.

*Preceding page*: Casa de Tierra–Catarina takes shape through interconnected structures of rammed earth, grounding the architecture in its site. Carved from the terrain, its color and texture echo the surrounding geology, reinforcing a deep connection to place.

*Left*: The outdoor dining terrace opens to a naturally landscaped garden by Hugo Sanchez, designed as an extension of the architecture. "For me, landscape is as important as architecture," says architect Héctor Barroso. "It must be in balance. Even when we intervene, it is done carefully and in dialogue with the architecture."

*Following pages, left*: The layout of the home allows for distinct spatial experiences. Custom shelving defines the living area and forms a transitional corridor to the stairwell, where a wood plinth and clay pot are sculptural elements.

*Following pages, right*: Framed openings throughout the house provide views of the surrounding trees and sky, reinforcing the architectural integration with nature. A restrained palette of neutral tones, exposed wood, and contemporary furnishings defines the interiors.

*Preceding pages*: This minimalist sanctuary honors its rural roots through a subdued palette and simple elegance. The interiors were designed and furnished by HABITACIÓN 116—a Mexico City-based design studio exploring traditional techniques and artisanal practices in a contemporary context, reinterpreting Mexico's cultural legacy through the lens of modern design.

*Left*: A muted palette infuses the wood-clad bedroom with a sense of calm, while a generous corner window opens to views of the garden.

*Following pages*: Mountain vistas unfold from the poolside living area, where volcanic stone fire pits encourage outdoor living year-round. A seamless transition between indoors and out is achieved through the continuous use of stone flooring.

*Right*: Casa de Tierra–Catarina rests gracefully within contemporary Mexican architecture. Borrowed from the land itself, the residence's rich tones mirror the surrounding mountain rock, offering a poetic dialogue between site and structure.

## Casa Santa Catarina / Emmanuel Picault

In rural Morelos, Emmanuel Picault's vision—a blend of modernist influences, vernacular motifs, and historic temples with echoes of brutalism—unfolds gradually, revealing an experimental retreat within the foothills of the rugged Tepozteco Mountains, just forty minutes from Mexico City. This deconstructed concrete weekend abode, home to the architect, designer, and founder of Chic by Accident, is rich with both whimsical nuances and an adventurous spirit.

Casa Santa Catarina, a concrete structure devoid of conventional boundaries, is less of a building and more a canvas of air, light, and shadows crafted for repose and contemplation. Essentially, the entire home, with its colonnaded terraces and absence of doors and windows, is assembled to create space for relaxation with one large indoor / outdoor space designed for leisure.

Influenced by "emotional architecture," a concept articulated by the artist Mathias Goeritz, Picault focuses on the sensory experience of architecture, prioritizing feelings, sounds, and textures in his designs. This philosophy is evident in the fluid, organic nature of the home's construction, which progresses based on his initial personal interactions with the site. Guided by intuition rather than formal blueprints, Picault's construction process exemplifies playful creativity. Employing unorthodox methods, including drawing a floor plan on the ground with a makeshift tool, he orchestrates a symphony of concrete, lime, and local stone.

Drawing from diverse cultural influences, Picault's architectural journey merges European modernism with Mesoamerican heritage. His reverence for historical sites as architectural marvels, rather than just relics, underscores an intense appreciation for the dialogue between history and contemporary design. The designer's initial exploration of Mexico's Aztec and Mayan legacies profoundly shaped his understanding of architecture, inspiring him to design houses as if they were temples—sacred spaces crafted from earth, stone, wood, and light.

His vision of the design unfolds organically, as he surrenders to the ebb and flow of inspiration. Within this evolving canvas, unexpected details emerge as poetic accents, from spherical stargazing platforms to Mayan-inspired artifacts integrated into the structure. The designer says that poetry, literature, and music create a deep and delicate territory of inspiration for his designs, and he likens the design of Casa Santa Catarina to a music composition, in which the tempo must relate to the composition as a whole, but also have the power to disturb the composition and create an element of surprise.

Picault is always collecting, so the home decor is a collage of happy accidents and objects found by chance that end up being centerpieces. Each element, whether reclaimed, or casually curated, embodies Picault's philosophy of welcoming chance and celebrating the beauty of imperfection.

Time is both muse and collaborator in this architectural odyssey. As the house weathers and ages, it acquires a distinctive patina, enhancing its character. The designer views this temporal evolution not as a detriment but as an ally, adding layers and stories that enrich the structure's narrative. He compares his design approach to weaving—adding elements over time without altering the fabric of the structure, resulting in a space that is perpetually evolving and never truly complete.

*Page 129*: Drawing from history and culture, architect and designer Emmanuel Picault approaches architecture through the framework of archaeology, viewing ancient sites not just as historical locations, but also as design references. His work layers natural materials—stone, earth, wood—and concrete with intentional light and shadow, evoking the structure and atmosphere of ancient temples and sacred spaces.

*Pages 130–31*: At the entrance, spherical platforms for stargazing signal the transition into the house. An exterior wall features Mayan-inspired sculptures created by architect Spero Daltas for the 1960 UDLA annex in Mexico City. Recontextualized here, they create a bold visual statement.

*Page 132*: The interiors are humble yet deliberate, grounded in the surrounding terrain and intended for relaxation and connection. Built over time, the stone structure reflects a philosophy of "slow architecture." Picault notes, "It's a house that may never be completed. I like the process of ongoing creation and the sense of freedom that comes with it."

*Page 133*: Stripped back to its essence—no doors, no windows, and minimal comforts—Casa Santa Catarina is a dwelling designed for rest and retreat, where openness defines the experience. The interior is a tapestry of time and place: mid-century pieces set beside neo-pre-Hispanic artifacts, indigenous crafts, and spontaneous totems—an alchemy Picault describes as chic by accident.

*Preceding pages*: Framed by the mountains near Tepoztlán's Pueblo Mágico, the unconventional weekend retreat is both sanctuary and experiment. The residence reinterprets modernist principles with local materials and references, integrating elements of brutalism and regional vernacular.

*Opposite*: Casa Santa Catarina wears its age with grace, open to the elements and resplendent with nature's visible patina. Its walls are a canvas for natural growth—mossy greens that speak to the building's integration with its environment and the passage of time.

## Casa Izar / Taller ADG

At a vertiginous altitude, on the undulating mountainous precipice of Valle de Bravo, with a breathtaking panorama of Lake Avándaro below, Casa Izar commands attention. Immersed in its surroundings, this impressive single-family residence by Alonso de Garay of Taller ADG is one of two twin houses designed for brothers.

Envisioned as an organic extension of the landscape, the architectural narrative is in symbiotic dialogue with the terrain. Native timber, local stone, and verdant vegetation coalesce to form an architectural feat that celebrates nature's raw beauty. Clad in a skin of wooden shingles and crowned with lush green rooftops, the sustainable structure melds with the natural wooded landscape.

Beyond its aesthetic appeal, Casa Izar champions environmental stewardship. By nurturing wetlands, creating recreational trails, and supporting a forest with many edible plants, the residence fosters biodiversity while minimizing its ecological footprint. Demonstrating ingenuity, the house boasts remarkable energy efficiency, harnessing natural light and rainwater to provide a living environment that upholds sustainability.

The journey into Casa Izar begins through an outdoor plaza adorned with regional stone and tranquil water features, merging with the lakeside. Negotiating the site's steep sloped topography, two distinct twin structures rise majestically, delineating private sanctuaries on the lower tier and communal spaces on the upper level.

Inside, the interior design, curated by Micaela de Bernardi, pays homage to the rugged splendor of the mountain locale. Finished with natural timber, and bathed in light via expansive windows, internal atriums, and skylights, the interiors exude inviting warmth. The living spaces feature bespoke furnishings by such design luminaries as Rick Owens and Yves Klein, along with sculptures by Pedro Reyes.

Designed for social gatherings, the terraces offer an immersive experience, with lounging areas framing views of the lake, the gray granite infinity pool, and landscaped gardens. Attention to detail is present in every facet of the design, ensuring that each space, whether indoor or out, offers a panorama of the tranquil lake waters below.

The residence rises above its architectural confines to become a haven where the rhythms of nature converge with the comforts of home. While showcasing a refined collection of both Mexican and international art and design, Casa Izar is a sophisticated example of sustainability and elegance, a symbol of how architecture can surpass mere living spaces to become sanctuaries that embrace both the natural environment and the inner sanctum of home life.

Christo and Jeanne-Claude

MONET
Michelangelo
Manual of Typography

*Page 139*: From above, Casa Izar is immersed in the forested mountainside overlooking Lake Avándaro in Valle de Bravo. Architect Alonso de Garay of ADG sought to weave the structure into the very fabric of the land. Clad in wood shingles and crowned with green rooftops, the sustainable home mirrors the terrain—its form shaped by the region's topography and the valley's enfolding hills.

*Preceding pages*: Tranquil lake views stretch from the living room across the gray granite pool toward the lake. A refined composition of art and design—a trio of stools by Rick Owens and a bold blue coffee table by Yves Klein—disrupt the neutral palette. Designer Micaela de Bernardi notes "Due to the space's generous dimensions, we sought to anchor the furniture to the earth through robust and low volumetry, predominately horizontal, as the lake is to the valley."

*Right*: Enveloped in rich timber, each room is envisioned as either an intimate container or a shared communal space. ADG sought to craft spaces that not only coexist with nature but also celebrate its beauty, inviting the inhabitants to feel as if they are part of a living, breathing ecosystem. As the seasons shift, so too does the experience of the home, its architecture responsive to nature's evolving palette.

*Following pages, left*: At the heart of the home, the central internal glassed garden rises through both levels, drawing in light and nurturing a continuous connection to the outdoors. The adjoining hall serves as a gallery, showcasing works by contemporary Mexican artists.

*Following pages, right*: At Izar, the atmosphere is one of unity, with rooms that nurture the spirit, allowing the residents to immerse themselves in nature's rhythms and find solace or connection.

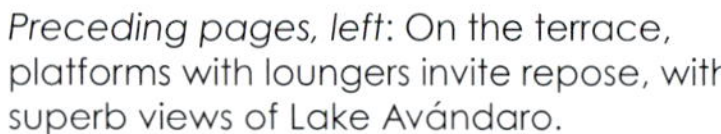

*Preceding pages, left*: On the terrace, platforms with loungers invite repose, with superb views of Lake Avándaro.

*Preceding pages, right*: A polyhedral form and granite path trace the geometry of the slender pool. Reflected in glass, nature speaks in constant dialogue with the landscape. "It's crucial that architecture roots itself in its environment; only then can it evoke a sense of belonging that transcends the physical structure," says de Garay.

*Right*: More than just a place of rest, the primary suite is a peaceful retreat with an open fireplace and sitting area, extending onto a private terrace overlooking the lake. Warm wood tones reference the surrounding woodland.

## La Colina Frente a la Cañada / HW Studio Arquitectos

Juxtaposed against the rugged terrain near Morelia, Michoacán, the Hill in Front of the Glen, or la Colina Frente a la Cañada, by HW Studio appears as a natural presence within its wooded mountainous landscape. This architectural endeavor, conceived by Rogelio Vallejo Bores, along with associates Oscar Didier Ascencio Castro and Nik Zaret, seeks not just to inhabit space, but also to enhance the inherent beauty of its environment.

Rejecting traditional labels such as "house," the architects aimed to create a structure that transcended conventional living spaces, aspiring instead to create a sophisticated, inventive retreat. This building, envisioned as a subterranean sanctuary, may be reclaimed by nature if ever abandoned in the future.

HW Studio envisioned a hidden getaway that would not only provide shelter but also engage the senses; the clients sought not merely a place to live, but a sensory experience as well—a weekend retreat, crafted to meld with its surroundings in a meaningful, almost spiritual manner.

The conceptual design was spurred by the site's beauty and the clients' willingness to embrace a distinctive architectural narrative. Fundamentally, the philosophy of the design questions the essence of shelter and explores the interplay of visibility and protection, inspired by the image of a child under a bedsheet—a universal symbol of simple comfort.

The structure is envisaged as a subtle punctuation in nature's ongoing prose; it seeks not to overshadow, but to complement. The low-slung construction partially dug into the ground integrates seamlessly with the terrain, mimicking the organic forms of the surrounding hills through strategic use of concrete. This material anchors the building to its site while also sculpting a new topography, blurring the lines between the manufactured and the natural.

Approaching the dwelling, one is drawn into a transformative journey along a narrow path, flanked by the undulating walls of the structure. This pathway, designed for solitary passage, leads to a lone tree, the architecture curving gently to acknowledge its ancient presence.

Inside, a concrete vault supports the green roof above, the cavernous space revealing raw textures of concrete and wood set against expansive views of the pine-studded landscape. The design is deliberately minimal, allowing each element—from the timber flooring to the furnishings handcrafted from locally-sourced wood—to speak for the forest itself.

Boundaries are dissolved between inside and out, with private areas opening to intimate courtyards, and views that capture the treetops and sky. This fluidity extends into the open public spaces and the dialogue the building enjoys with the environment, ensuring that it remains a part of the landscape it respects so deeply.

The structure is designed to evolve over time, its concrete form gradually blending with the forest's organic elements. It is envisioned to age gracefully, acquiring a layer of moss and the rough texture of bark, becoming an intrinsic part of the environment it was designed to honor.

This project by HW Studio is an ode to the enduring beauty of nature, a thoughtful insertion into land that forms a new hill. The Hill in Front of the Glen, is a poetic reflection on what it means to live in harmony with our surroundings, both now and in the future.

*Page 151*: A silent gesture in concrete and earth, this home by HW Studio reads like an architectural poem—written in the language of the land. Partially submerged into the wooded mountainside, it blurs the line between built form and terrain.

*Preceding pages, left*: In the kitchen, a monolithic concrete island integrates the sink and stovetop beneath a sculptural steel lamp by HW Studio. A long wooden cabinet adds warmth, connecting the kitchen to the dining area in a single, continuous space.

*Preceding pages, right*: Conceived with reverence for the site, the project is both a sanctuary and a seamless extension of its natural surroundings. Linear planes intersect with the home's curved shell, opening to the forest. The dining table's single steel slab complements the restrained palette.

*Opposite*: Aligned with HW Studio's commitment to sustainability and ensuring the furniture blends seamlessly with the architecture, the furnishings create cohesive and integrated interiors. Clean lines and geometric forms contrast with the sweeping curve of the concrete ceiling. Timber, sourced from the surrounding forest, enhances the connection to place, while a custom concrete fireplace with a steel hood grounds the living space.

*Following pages, left*: The hall, framed by concrete walls, guides visitors into the home through the front door, continuing a silent procession from the entry path.

*Following pages, right*: The layout balances openness and seclusion. Social spaces face the ravine; bedrooms open to a sheltered courtyard. A built-in concrete bed, wood floors, and a wood bench create a serene, tactile atmosphere.

*Pages 158–59*: Following the curve of the hillside, the architecture envelops like a mantle—protective, quiet, and deeply rooted in its setting. Tucked into the rear, three bedrooms offer refuge, defined by raw concrete beds, wooden trunks, and minimal steel clothing rails.

*Page 160*: The house's design resembles a gentle hill, partially submerged, blending subtly with its natural surroundings.

*Page 161*: Drawing inspiration from the landscape, the house invites a sensory journey. The entry path curves inward, narrowing as it approaches a solitary tree, where a subtle bend in the wall makes space for passage.

## Casa Tepetate / Manuel Cervantes Studio

Tepetate, by Manuel Cervantes Studio, derives its name from the characteristic reddish limestone prevalent in Mexico's volcanic terrain. This distinctive hue, integrated into the property's pigmented concrete partitions, provides a rich, earthy canvas that complements the lush greenery enveloping the residence.

Spanning more than eight thousand square feet, two concrete structures are arranged in a Latin cross configuration across two primary levels. Three patios dictate the home's layout, each oriented to foster a connection between the indoor spaces and the surrounding landscape. As the property ascends toward a natural ravine at its boundary, the architectural composition strategically gains elevation, enhancing its presence and integrating it with the terrain.

The interior of the home centers around the courtyard patios, designed around three existing trees preserved through innovative platforms safeguarding their roots. These trees not only accentuate the architectural narrative, but also dictate the flow of natural light and ventilation throughout the residence. This consideration is crucial as parts of the home are below street level, necessitating a sensitive design to optimize light and airflow.

From the main entrance, the communication with the outdoors is immediately apparent. A grand interior patio, bordered by masonry crafted from local volcanic stone, guides visitors from the entryway through the main staircase into the sublime sanctuary. This path not only serves a functional purpose but also enhances the dialogue between architectural repetition and variation that Cervantes champions.

Inside, the design of Casa Tepetate continues to pay homage to its environment. Ceilings featuring ribbed concrete extend throughout, creating a rhythmic, linear pattern that introduces a rustic touch to this urban dwelling designed for a young family. This architectural feature resonates with the home's robust external forms and the grittiness of its surroundings.

Dedicated rooms within the house embrace botanical themes. A green atrium in the kitchen and a botanical atelier echo the concept of an internal garden. This design explores the interplay of vegetation in shaded and enclosed settings, creating a tranquil, contemplative environment. The use of flooring of timber and recinto negro, a local black volcanic stone, reinforces the home's connection to its setting.

Cervantes's approach extends beyond architectural design to engage deeply with the cultural and material heritage of Mexico. His work is not merely about constructing spaces but about crafting environments that resonate with the local context and heritage. The meticulous selection of materials and the incorporation of traditional Mexican craftsmanship reflect a commitment to celebrating and preserving cultural identity within a contemporary framework.

Tepetate presents a modern tribute to Mexican architecture, where every element—from the structural to the decorative—serves as a subtle nod acknowledging the country's rich history and culture. Manuel Cervantes Studio has created an elegant, contemporary canvas capturing the essence of its locale, highlighting both innovation in design and the enduring beauty of nature.

*Preceding page*: Located in Mexico City, Casa Tepetate draws from the distinctive reddish limestone found in the area.

*Opposite*: The architecture by Manuel Cervantes Studio unfolds through layered surfaces of clay-colored concrete, wood, and volcanic stone, leading through a series of courtyards that gradually transition from public to private spaces.

*Following pages, left*: Warm tones, tactile materials, and thoughtful details shape the interiors. In the kitchen, an atrium introduces a living layer of greenery to the architectural composition.

*Following pages, right*: The residence presents a nuanced study in texture and transparency. Earth-toned surfaces and handcrafted details enrich the open-plan interiors, while courtyards seamlessly integrate the built environment with the natural surroundings.

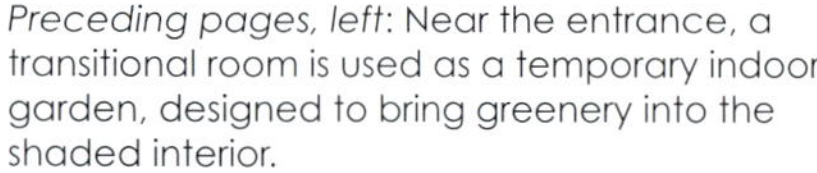

*Preceding pages, left*: Near the entrance, a transitional room is used as a temporary indoor garden, designed to bring greenery into the shaded interior.

*Preceding pages, right*: A serene sanctuary, the primary bedroom, enclosed in warm wood finishes, offers a calm retreat. A sitting area overlooks the adjacent garden, abundant with natural light and greenery. A round concrete table and pottery add simple focal points.

*Right*: Concrete and wood create contrast and warmth. Furnishings are contemporary as well as minimal, shaped to reflect local design traditions. The space is open, functional, and grounded in material clarity.

MÉXICO 200 AÑOS

*Opposite*: An internal secret garden inspired by Luis Barragán welcomes light and nature into the home. Vintage furnishings and contemporary artworks transform the living area into a hybrid space—part salon, part gallery—anchored by architectural clarity.

*Following pages*: Sculptures, textiles, and works by Pedro Reyes populate the space, which opens directly onto a verdant courtyard—a convergence of art, architecture, and landscape.

*Opposite*: A monolithic table, cylindrical pendant lamp, and sculptural chairs—all designed by Reyes—define the kitchen as an extension of the studio. The composition emphasizes material weight and form, oriented toward the adjacent courtyard garden.

*Following pages, left*: At the entrance, a sculpture by Reyes introduces color and texture, a contrast to the black stone floor and concrete architecture.

*Following pages, right*: Reyes's sculptures and architecture draw inspiration from brutalism, Mexican modernism, and Mesoamerican history, architecture, and art. Geometric sculptures, formed from stone and volcanic basalt pay homage to ancient traditions and cultures. "The process starts at the quarry, where I select the stones that I will be taking to the studio. Each stone has elements that are halfway to a sculpture," says Reyes.

*Right*: Sculpted forms as functional objects. A carved volcanic stone handbasin and bathtub, present as sculptural installations.

## Estudio Graciela Iturbide / Taller de Arquitectura Mauricio Rocha + Gabriela Carrillo

Rising over a vibrant local neighborhood in Mexico City, a three-story clay tower ascends. This deconstructed building, conceived by Taller de Arquitectura Mauricio Rocha + Gabriela Carrillo, was designed for Rocha's mother, celebrated Mexican photographer Graciela Iturbide. Constructed entirely of exposed red bricks—a traditional element in Mexican architecture—this edifice serves as both studio and residence.

This commission holds personal significance for Mauricio Rocha, the son of Iturbide and architect Manuel Rocha Diaz, who began his own career in architecture "to provide a response to the place in which we live, our places, our economic and social situations," and to "translate the traditions and materials of the places in which we operate in a contemporary way, not through fashionable forms or fireworks, but with silence, space, the experience of emptiness."

Rocha embarked on his architectural trajectory aiming to craft spaces reflective of their geographic and cultural contexts, aspiring to reinterpret local traditions and materials through a contemporary lens, eschewing fleeting trends for designs characterized by tranquility and appreciation of negative space.

The building's design emphasizes serenity and fluidity, featuring three vertically aligned configurations crafted solely from bricks, eliminating the need for steel or concrete supports. The interior walls integrate bookshelves and other necessities seamlessly, preserving the uninterrupted geometry of the space. The two internal courtyard patios enlivened with cacti and indigenous plants provide subtle visual breaks in the monochromatic scheme, which emphasizes the precise, clean lines throughout.

Inside, the brick walls are enlivened by the interplay of cast light that filters through small openings, cracks, and crevices, forging a connection between the interior and the exterior. The enclosed courtyards and rooftop terrace, lush and meticulously maintained by Iturbide, echo her deep engagement with the essence of everyday life, captured in her predominantly black-and-white photography held in numerous collections, including the San Francisco Museum of Modern Art and the Getty Museum.

Iturbide's artistic focus lies in the deep exploration of her cultural milieu, as she seeks to comprehend the multifaceted tapestry that is Mexico. Her poetic images tell stories of indigenous Mexican cultures and societal transformations, with a focus on themes of identity, ritual, and the female experience.

This building is fundamentally a search for silence, a quest for simplicity and a continuous, rhythmic repetition of a single material. It is a structure capable of simultaneously exuding both a rich warmth and feelings of bare essentiality, embodying the spirit and creativity of its inhabitant through an innovative approach to traditional materials and form.

*Page 191*: A sculptural tower of red brick rises above the surrounding vernacular architecture of Mexico City's historic Coyoacán district.

*Preceding pages*: The building evokes a sense of calm and spatial continuity. Anchored by internal courtyards on either side, the clay structure is enveloped in lush greenery—private oases that dissolve the boundary between built form and nature.

*Opposite*: The architecture exudes a spirit of openness and creative liberation. Conceived by Mauricio Rocha as part studio, part home for his mother, renowned photographer Graciela Iturbide, the building becomes an extension of the artist's work. A black-and-white framed photograph by the artist leans against the wall.

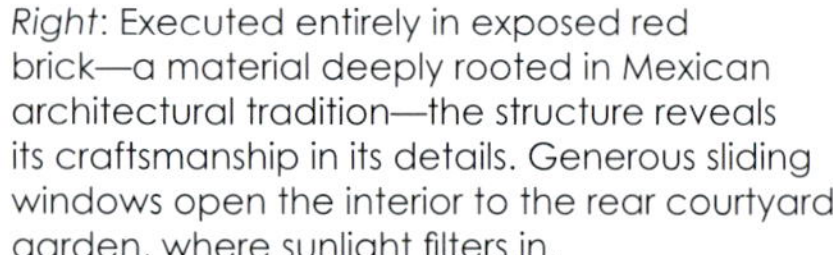

*Right*: Executed entirely in exposed red brick—a material deeply rooted in Mexican architectural tradition—the structure reveals its craftsmanship in its details. Generous sliding windows open the interior to the rear courtyard garden, where sunlight filters in.

*Following pages, left*: Functional elements are seamlessly integrated into the architecture; bookshelves and services are embedded within the walls, allowing the purity of the space to remain undisturbed. Metal retablos are set on a clay wall.

*Following pages, right*: On the rooftop terrace, sculptural potted cacti provide a striking contrast to the red clay structure.

## Casa Estudio / Manuel Cervantes Studio

Manuel Cervantes's Casa Estudio, a masterful blend of luxury and functionality, presents a striking example of modern Mexican architecture. Located in Mexico City's Lomas de Chapultepec, this five-story structure, both a family home and a design studio, steps down a steep hillside, offering panoramic views from each level. The design forms a staggered structure, generating a series of terraces, serving as an extension of the interior space at each level. This thoughtful design integrates the building seamlessly into its unique urban setting, a steep, lush ravine encircled by a valley and flanked by distant volcanoes. Cervantes's philosophy emphasizes creating projects deeply rooted in their geographical and cultural contexts, a principle that is manifested impressively in Casa Estudio.

Using environmental characteristics of the site as an architectural reference and starting point, the structure preserves and highlights the surrounding natural elements. Materials used in the construction are integral to the region. Locally sourced elements—rich walnut wood, lava stone concrete, and ceramic brick—provide the house with a profound sense of place and history. The thoughtfully-chosen materials not only reflect the local environment but also enhance the building's tactile and visual appeal.

A steep staircase leads to Cervantes's design studio, housed in a striking almost sixteen-foot-high concrete structure with a glazed rear wall overlooking the verdant ravine. This space was conceived as a "window to his work," where clients can witness the creative process and gain a deeper understanding of his design philosophy. The studio's austere palette, featuring board-formed concrete walls and ceiling, and dark lava stone floors, provides a dramatic backdrop for the architectural models on display. Cervantes eschews the conventional office layout in favor of a more intimate, domestic atmosphere where ideas can flourish away from the distractions of everyday life.

Ascending to the next level reveals a sophisticated social area. One of the most striking features here is the series of floor-to-ceiling glazed panels that pivot open, seamlessly merging the indoor space with the outdoor environment. Cervantes explains that his design process starts with the garden, which sets the tone for the rest of the house. The Mexican climate allows for this open connection, blurring the boundaries between interior and exterior spaces. Natural light and ventilation play key roles in the home's design, with expansive windows spanning entire walls. An interior garden atrium near the dining room, featuring a ceramic brick wall, brings an additional touch of nature into the home.

Throughout the residence, the consistent use of materials and the corresponding color palette create a cohesive aesthetic. Utilitarian concrete and ceramic brick juxtaposed with the warmth of wood adds a layer of richness to the family spaces. These areas are filled with an eclectic mix of books, artifacts, and contemporary Mexican design, reflecting Cervantes's penchant for collecting items with personal significance. His home serves as a repository of memories, showcasing objects and relics from his travels and walks in nature, reflecting his diverse interests and experiences.

Casa Estudio is a tangible expression of Cervantes's architectural ideology. Each element of the home—from its strategic use of materials to its seamless integration with the natural surroundings—reflects his dedication to creating spaces that are intrinsically linked to their environment and cultural context. This thoughtful approach to design not only enriches the living experience but also fosters a deeper connection to the heritage and vibrant landscape of Mexico City.

*Page 201*: Mexican architect Manuel Cervantes's Casa Estudio in Mexico City is both his private family home and work studio and merges Mexican culture within a natural urban setting.

*Preceding pages, left*: The entry sequence unfolds in light and shadow. Walnut, lava stone, ceramic and concrete brick, and textured concrete panels layer warmth and depth, while recinto negro basalt anchors the structure in its volcanic terrain.

*Preceding pages, right*: The studio, carved into an almost sixteen-foot-high concrete space, opens fully to a lush ravine through a glazed rear facade. Within, an austere palette serves as a contemplative backdrop for the architect's creative process.

*Opposite*: The dining area with its distinctive wood ceiling, extends to a patio suspended over the ravine. An internal atrium brings nature inside.

*Following pages*: Glazed panels pivot to dissolve boundaries between interior and landscape. Curated objects and contemporary Mexican design reveal a narrative of place and memory. For Cervantes, true luxury lies in the intimacy of shared moments.

*Page 208*: Tactile wood and stone surfaces, a chiaroscuro of light and dark, create a sense of depth and volume in the kitchen.

*Page 209*: Unfolding onto a roof terrace, the bedroom reinforces the interiors' understated elegance.

Gabriel Figueroa

ANDO
DALI

## La Platanera / Alberto Kalach

In Mexico City, hidden behind a nondescript urban facade amidst a serene enclave of courtyard gardens and secluded banana groves, is La Platanera, the residence renovated and designed by Alberto Kalach for gallerists Mónica Manzutto and José Kuri. This structure seamlessly integrates restored brick edifices with modern construction, creating a dialogue between historical references and contemporary idioms.

The story of La Platanera, which was built in 1899 as a nunnery near the church of San Miguel Arcángel, is a tale of transformation. Under Kalach's intervention and the stewardship of Manzutto and Kuri, the structure transcends its original colonial beginnings and clerical use. Renamed after the banana trees in its garden, the house celebrates the passage of time, its aging facade attesting to the layers of history within its walls.

The urban home, designed for the founders and owners of the nearby Galeria Kurimanzutto (also designed by Kalach), unveils a mysterious sequence of garden spaces, enriched with sunlight and vibrant vegetation. From the street, a modest door in an unassuming wall grants entry to a garden that serves as a living room, adorned with a fur hammock and a cozy sofa arrangement. This courtyard, paved with black stone and surrounded by lush tropical plants, presents a unique blend of nature and culture. It is an outdoor space that simultaneously functions as an interior, merging the boundaries between inside and outside.

Kalach is known for his meticulous attention to detail and reverence for both Mexican modernism and traditional Japanese carpentry. His designs pay homage to the architectural philosophies of pre-Hispanic Mexico by balancing mass and void and merging the indoor with the outdoor, enhancing the sensory and spatial experience.

Substantial renovations have preserved the nuns' quarters, while ruins have been integrated and reimagined as enclosed garden spaces and other areas have been transformed into gardens. Exhibiting great respect for the house's rich history and significance, the architect creates a layered, loosely organized layout around the courtyard and small, interconnected rooms. Each room—whether a kitchen, dining area, office, or reading nook—opens toward the central courtyard.

The only completely new additions are the two buildings at the garden's rear. Behind the banana trees, amidst a stand of bamboo, is a detached wooden pavilion with a separate modern structure crafted from concrete, steel, and glass that houses private sleeping quarters. This area opens to a forecourt with a native tepozán tree—a striking emblem of resilience and continuity.

La Platanera makes an insightful statement about cultural heritage, reflecting the principles of Kurimanzutto and the gallery's contributions to both local and international art narratives. In its eclectic and refined essence, the residence presents an example of cultural pride and innovative living, embodying a fusion of tradition and modernity that is uniquely Mexican.

Kalach envisioned and conceived a house of quiet beauty and significance without seeking to make a grand statement. It is the antithesis of ostentation, blending seamlessly with its surroundings. Its richness, with rooms that speak of decay and renewal, unfolds in an inward world, devoid of formal representation to the city. This is a dwelling where gardens transform into rooms and rooms into gardens, blurring the lines between them. The essence of La Platanera lies in this tropical intuition and in architectural interventions that honor the site's cultural heritage.

AVANT-GARDES

*Page 211*: La Platanera is the Mexico City home of gallerists Mónica Manzutto and José Kuri. A recent addition by architect Alberto Kalach introduces a bedroom suite, immersed in native vegetation.

*Pages 212–13*: A detached pavilion rests among bamboo and banana trees, barely perceptible within the garden's layered canopy. The office pavilion, surrounded by dense foliage, is a place of work and a welcome retreat.

*Pages 214–15*: Banana groves—platanera translates to banana grove—surround the wood-clad structure, lending the residence its name. A path winds through lush greenery, linking the home's disparate spaces.

*Preceding pages, left*: In the garden, a pink iron table, set amongst a verdant backdrop, punctuates the landscape with playful color. Architectural remnants have been reimagined as walled gardens, where art and nature cohabit.

*Preceding pages, right*: La Platanera is a dialogue between past and present—restored brick ruins merge seamlessly with contemporary forms, creating a residence poised between nature and civilization.

*Right*: The gallery-like entry with a wooden bench, pops of color, and art.

LOUIS VUITTON
002

CONTEMPORARY HOUSES
LUXURY HOTELS
1,000 PLACES TO SEE BEFORE YOU DIE
DIAMONDS
Tom Kundig
CHANEL
GRAY MALI
TOM FORD
CONTEMPORARY HOUSES
Architecture in the 20th Century
bauhaus

*Opposite*: Wood and concrete frame the lower level, welcoming greenery into the architecture.

*Following pages, left*: A sculptural staircase spirals upward through the center of the home—an architectural gesture of fluidity and material elegance.

*Following pages, right*: Cocooned in rich tones of timber, the primary bedroom exudes restrained luxury.

## Casa Mezcal / Barde vanVoltt

Casa Mezcal appears as a paragon of Mexican design, where art, furniture, and craftsmanship converge in an opus inspired by mezcal—the venerable Mexican spirit distilled from the agave plant.

Realized by the Mexico-based Dutch interior design and architecture firm Barde vanVoltt, the space retains its original identity as a mezcal tasting room. Central to the indoor patio is a terra-cotta bar, seamlessly integrated into the environment. Here, beneath the branches of a seventeen-foot tall *guayabo Japonés* tree and a retractable glass roof, the setting is a convivial gathering spot.

Prior to the transformation, Bart van Seggelen and Valérie Boerma of Barde vanVoltt discerned the raw potential and intrinsic spirit of the space. Their design ethos meticulously blends historical and modern elements, preserving the authenticity of the original art deco steel windows while artfully replicating them throughout the space to enhance the continuity between rooms. A sculptural staircase, finished in clay tile, brings warmth and tactility with its graceful form. Overhead, a custom chandelier by Studio David Pompa accentuates the space with small spheres of light.

The metamorphosis of Casa Mezcal into a verdant sanctuary in the heart of Condesa, Mexico City, is furthered by the introduction of a serene color palette. Echoing nature's hues, the palette incorporates agave green, delicate terra-cotta, and chukum stucco, all juxtaposed against the textural backdrop of gray concrete. This design reconfigures the three-story layout around two garden courtyards, fostering natural ventilation and blending indoor and outdoor spaces. The collaboration with local landscape studio Aldaba Jardines enriches this dialogue, creating a serene oasis amidst the urban expanse.

Within Casa Mezcal, each element reverberates with the rich cultural heritage of Mexico. Barde vanVoltt's designs, encompassing custom furnishings, lighting, and tiles come to life through collaborations with local artisans. Art plays a central role throughout, resonating both within the residence and beyond, complementing the minimalist aesthetics and refined details characteristic of Barde vanVoltt's designs.

The residence is a celebration of traditional craftsmanship and contemporary design, a tapestry woven together by history and modernity. Casa Mezcal represents its cultural context, offering a vibrant interplay of history, culture, design, and art—in a soulful narrative and evocative chapter in the building's evolution.

*Preceding page*: Reimagined by Mexico City–based studio Barde vanVoltt, Casa Mezcal is a thoughtful restoration that bridges heritage and modernity in Mexico City's Condesa neighborhood.

*Right*: Traditional forms meet contemporary restraint in the kitchen, where arched openings promote natural airflow. A sculptural pendant lamp by Studio David Pompa anchors the space with understated drama.

*Following pages*: An evocative composition of contemporary Mexican design, the living space features a custom velvet sofa, handwoven rug, and artisanal lighting—each element contributing to the narrative of craft and place.

*Page 240*: Muted colors lead through an arched portal toward the Mezcal bar and open-air patio.

*Page 241*: Once a Mezcal tasting room, this patio is now a central pavilion that honors the house's legacy. A guava tree rises beneath a retractable glass ceiling, inviting the outdoors in.

*Preceding pages, left*: Arches recall the building's art deco origins. A handmade chair by Roberto Michelsen subtly nods to Gerrit Rietveld's iconic geometry.

*Preceding pages, right*: A sculpted brutalist-inspired staircase, with steps finished in clay, adds warmth and tactility. Overhead, a custom chandelier by Studio David Pompa, made with opal frosted glass and fiorito stone quarried in Puebla, accentuates the space.

*Left*: A partition of hand-formed Oaxacan bricks fuses tradition with bold material expression.

## Casa Escuela / Ezequiel Farca & Mónica Calderón

Casa Escuela, an unexpected synthesis of the remnants of a colonial schoolhouse, ancient Mayan gardens, and contemporary design interventions, demonstrates an extraordinary narrative of architectural rebirth. Originally constructed in 1919 in Mérida, the hacienda transitioned from a private residence to a primary school, and was later abandoned. Architect Ezequiel Farca and designer Mónica Calderón embarked on this passion project, a four-year-long journey, to revive this architectural jewel. Their vision transformed the property into both a personal family residence and a vibrant, multidisciplinary space, imbuing the structure with renewed vitality and purpose.

Central to Farca and Calderón's vision was the thoughtful preservation of the building's historical integrity. The intricate pasta-tile floors and exposed wooden beams were restored with meticulous attention. These historical features are combined with contemporary elements, creating a fluid dialogue between the old and the new.

In their homage to both sustainability and local heritage, Farca and Calderón selected natural, locally-sourced materials, taking inspiration from the ancient stonework and construction techniques of Mexico's indigenous cultures. Collaborating with skilled artisans, they crafted bespoke design elements that infuse the space with unique character and depth. Utilizing concrete bricks and custom-made breeze blocks along with bioclimatic design principles, Farca and Calderón have reinterpreted the traditional colonial home through a modern lens.

The extension features walls evoking *sacbeob*, the ancient white roads of the Mayans, and integrates bespoke iron and glass doors along with stone pavers that merge indoor and outdoor spaces. This thoughtful design extends into the interiors, where the serene living area contrasts with a vibrant yellow kitchen, echoing Luis Barragán's famous use of color.

Furnishings are a blend of contemporary pieces crafted by Farca and Calderón, complemented by classics from design luminaries Jean Prouvé and Charlotte Perriand. The interior showcases artworks and objects predominantly by Mexican artists, reflecting the couple's dedication to local talent. Resin vessels by Mónica Calderón Studio and Mexican Mestiz rugs, inspired by the nearby archaeological site and Mayan temple, Uxmal, infuse the home with a contemporary yet historic aesthetic.

The core of Casa Escuela is its courtyard, a versatile space with sculptures by notable artists which serves various functions, from hosting social gatherings to providing a serene retreat from the tropical heat.

Casa Escuela transcends the notion of a mere dwelling, serving also as a cultural epicenter where art, design, cuisine, hospitality, and wellness converge. The residence serves as a bridge between the past and the future, proving the power of a successful architectural reinvention. Casa Escuela pays tribute to the rich cultural mosaic of Mérida and the Yucatán peninsula—a place where history is not merely preserved but celebrated as a dynamic part of contemporary life.

*Page 247*: Once a forgotten nineteenth-century schoolhouse, Casa Escuela has been transformed into a private home and multidisciplinary retreat by architect Ezequiel Farca and designer Mónica Calderón. The original colonial structure was restored and expanded with a contemporary wing, blending tradition with modern living.

*Preceding pages, left*: A custom wall of breeze blocks frames the pool, filtering light and air. Crafted from native materials using regional techniques, it reflects the studio's commitment to local craftsmanship and climate-conscious design.

*Preceding pages, right*: In the bar area, natural textures and a muted palette create a calm, grounded setting. Irregularly stacked bricks add depth and tactility, reinforcing the home's earthy elegance.

*Right*: The living spaces celebrate the culture of the Yucatán Peninsula. Furnishings designed by the couple sit beside traditional crafts and iconic pieces, including a cabinet by Jean Prouvé and a door by Charlotte Perriand, displayed as sculpture.

RATIONAL

*Left:* Mustard-yellow kitchen cabinetry contrasts with ancient stone and chukum stucco walls. Former classrooms now serve as domestic spaces, layered with century-old character.

*Right*: After years of restoration, the dining room regained its original character and now, traditional tiles and heritage elements balance the introduction of clean, modern lines. Tall glass doors open to the pool and patio courtyard.

*Following pages, left*: In the bedroom, gray floor tiles extend to the custom bedframe and headboard, visually grounding the space. The breeze block screen filters sunlight, creating intricate patterns of light and shadow.

*Following pages, right*: Furnishings are chosen with restraint—sculptural chairs, a minimalist lamp, and artwork in the bedroom give presence without excess.

## Casa Monte / Carlos H. Matos

Situated on the Oaxacan Coast, set between the rugged contours of mountains and the serene expanse of the Pacific, Casa Monte emerges as a distinct presence amid the tapestry of cacti and resilient shrubs. It appears both a part of and apart from the encircling greenery, resembling a sanctuary gradually revealed by time—a coastal relic or temple that nature has only partially claimed.

This extraordinary shelter, designed by Carlos H. Matos for Claudio Sodi, merges the essences of architecture and sculpture. It serves as a contemporary tribute to the layers of history that are part of Mexico's architectural landscape through the twentieth century—a tribute to eras both distant and recent, whose influences are still felt today.

Alluding to Diego Rivera's conception of Anahuacalli as a modern ruin of sorts, the structure is a bold declaration of openness. There is an absence of windows and doors, dissolving the barriers between inside and out. The floor is a raised platform, domesticating a portion of the wild terrain. Robust columns and walls rise to craft not just a shelter but an architectural statement where the very notion of a house is reimagined as an expansive portico, reminiscent of a Roman bathhouse, complete with an indoor pool that refreshes the space.

Constructed from more than fifteen thousand concrete blocks, referencing the red earth of the nearby mountains, the edifice stands as a fundamentally sculptural form, evoking the legacy of past civilizations while hinting at futuristic ideals. The austere spaces, reminiscent of a cave or a friar's retreat, are severe yet serene, designed to be interacted with as a living sculpture. The facade's upper portion, textured with ribbed brittle formwork, recalls the thatched roofs of pre-Hispanic structures.

In a thoughtful homage to architectural history, Matos integrates elements reminiscent of Mexico's archaeological sites and iconic architectural epochs. His designs within the home pay tribute to such luminaries as Juan O'Gorman, Carlos Obregón Santacilia, and Frank Lloyd Wright during his Mayan revival period. Sunlight filters onto a wall relief by Matos, inspired by O'Gorman's murals, depicting a regional deity in the form of a ritualistic crab—an emblem of local culture.

The ground level encourages fluid interaction with the outdoors, fostering a connection with the elements. Ascending to the upper floor via a spiral staircase, one finds a secluded solitary space—a sleeping area designed as a protective sanctuary, where one can retreat and find tranquility. The use of ribbed brittle formwork on the exterior continues, paying homage to ancestral techniques and materials, while Matos's approach continues to blur the line between architecture and sculpture. A visionary creation, Casa Monte is a timeless refuge that offers both solace and an opportunity for contemplation within its sculptural confines.

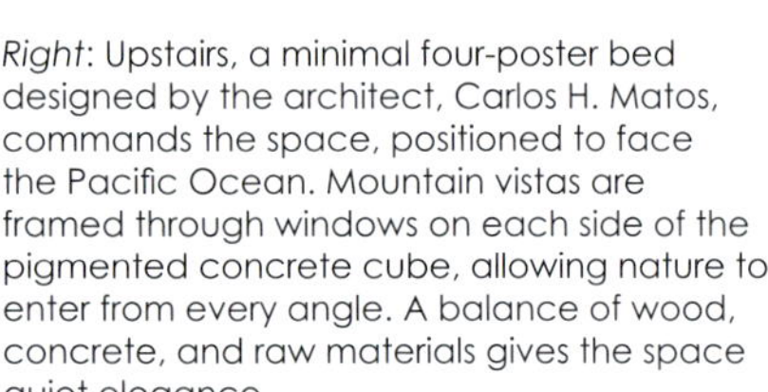

*Right*: Upstairs, a minimal four-poster bed designed by the architect, Carlos H. Matos, commands the space, positioned to face the Pacific Ocean. Mountain vistas are framed through windows on each side of the pigmented concrete cube, allowing nature to enter from every angle. A balance of wood, concrete, and raw materials gives the space quiet elegance.

*Following pages*: Casa Monte stands alone, embraced by native flora—an architectural relic or sacred monument gazing west toward the Pacific and east to the Sierra Mountains. A modern temple rooted in ancient memory.

*Preceding page*: Boulders act as stepping stones, leading to the entrance of the beach house, a project by Aranza de Ariño. Sculptural and elemental, they mark a slow approach into the architecture. The low-lying concrete structure sits directly on the sand, surrounded by dry tropical forest.

*Left*: Separate living areas are organized along a linear path, divided by open-air walkways. A mature ceiba tree and native plantings form part of the architecture, shaping space, offering privacy, and reinforcing the boundary between built and unbuilt.

*Right*: Though compact, the house offers all necessary comforts—its reduced footprint encourages a pared-back lifestyle aligned with its remote setting. Designed as a place of retreat, the interiors are minimal and deliberate to encourage solitude. Furnishings are kept to a minimum—only what is essential is here.

*Left*: The architecture defers to its setting, allowing nature to lead. The house invites stillness. Interior spaces open onto sand, forest, and garden. Shuttered louvered openings frame views and filter light.

*Following pages*: Resting lightly in the sand, with carefully placed openings, the long and low structure emerges from the dense vegetation. Facing the Sierra Mountains, the architecture avoids ocean views in favor of a closer connection to the land.

## Casa Naila / BAAQ

Positioned on the rocky shores of a slender peninsula in Oaxaca, Casa Naila engages in a thoughtful dialogue between architecture and the rugged beauty of the Pacific coastline. Designed by the architectural studio BAAQ, this unassuming beach house is a celebration of its environment, conceived to integrate its proximity to the ocean into every aspect of its design.

The beach retreat is artfully composed of four angular pavilions organized in a cross-shaped layout around a central courtyard. Large boulders along the shoreline informed the placement and proportion of the pavilions, which appear to float on concrete platforms, achieving a delicate balance with their natural surroundings. The orientation of each building assures ocean views from every room.

Local materials and simple construction methods, integral to the design, reflect the rural architectural traditions of Oaxaca. Floors are crafted from concrete mixed with local clay and earth, and perimeter walls are clad in slatted palm wood. This material, traditionally used in simple local beach huts, is reinterpreted here to add a layer of modernity while maintaining ecological sensitivity. The palm wood framework offers transparency for views and cross-ventilation, casting dramatic shadows by day, and transforms the building into a guiding point of light against the dark ocean by night.

Casa Naila is a fitting homage to Oaxaca, not only in its use of indigenous materials and techniques, but also in how it influences the experience of its inhabitants. Named after a beloved Oaxacan folksong, the house is a manifestation of BAAQ and its founding architect Alfonso Quiñones's philosophy of forging a deep connection between architecture and its site. His approach, influenced by his work experience with architects Tadao Ando and Álvaro Siza, is vividly realized in Casa Naila, presenting a model of how modern architecture can respect and enhance both the natural environment and local culture.

*Page 279*: Located on the coast of Oaxaca, Casa Naila is positioned directly on the sandy shore. The project by BAAQ centers on a shared courtyard and swimming pool, arranged around four distinct structures. A reclaimed wooden log acts as a footbridge linking the pavilions.

*Preceding pages*: The living area, oriented toward the ocean, integrates construction methods and materials common to the region. Floors are poured concrete mixed with clay and earth, producing a warm, tactile surface. The framework is made from palm wood traditionally used in simple coastal structures, reinterpreted here as operable screens that manage light, airflow, and privacy, adapted for a contemporary context.

*Opposite*: The kitchen is composed of a single, cast-in-place concrete block that combines open shelving and a cooktop into a unified element. A minimal staircase provides vertical circulation to the upper level, maintaining simplicity and continuity of materials.

*Following pages, left*: The bedroom's palm wood framework filters daylight, casting linear shadows that shift throughout the day. This detail functions both as solar control and a consistent architectural motif across the project.

*Following pages, right*: The architecture is shaped by its coastal context and constructed with a restrained, site-specific material palette. The buildings are elevated on concrete platforms to protect against shifting sand and water.

*Pages 286–87*: At dusk, the architecture settles into the landscape, catching the last light in its textured surfaces. The house moves between enclosure and openness. Its form is both elemental and precise—a response to site, climate, and tradition.

## Casa Altanera / TAC

Architect Alberto Calleja has masterfully blended brutalism with traditional Mexican craftsmanship in designing this award-winning beachfront holiday home for his family on an unspoiled segment of Mexico's Oaxaca Coast. This striking construction, known as Casa Altanera, not only encapsulates a modern aesthetic but also effortlessly immerses itself within its natural surroundings.

South of Puerto Escondido, a once-tranquil surf village now transformed into a vibrant art and architecture community—largely due to the Tadao Ando-designed Casa Wabi Foundation—the beach retreat sits secluded, accessible at the end of a simple dirt track. Its solid brutalist forms, comprised of identical concrete structures and a thatched roof pavilion, are juxtaposed against bramble and hills of cacti.

The residence is crafted using natural materials and age-old techniques, underscoring the architect's intention to foster a profound connection with the coastal landscape. Under a large, open-air thatched pavilion facing the ocean, the living, dining, and kitchen spaces extend out to the pool deck. Retractable wooden doors open wide to the ocean, inviting cool breezes and offering expansive views of the sea and landscape, where fishermen and local cowboys are regular sights.

Measuring four thousand square feet, the house is segmented into three distinct buildings, with social areas in the main space, and the main suite and guest bedrooms in separate pavilions, each operating independently. Wooden walkways and outdoor pathways linking the structures together weave around dry tropical vegetation, dotted with cacti.

The architectural philosophy of Taller Alberto Calleja (TAC) revolves around intuitively creating spaces for encounter and exchange, spaces that evoke emotion, while embedding these structures within their context. This philosophy is clear in Casa Altanera, where architecture not only meets but also enhances the landscape. The architect's commitment to the natural environment extends beyond construction; a reforestation initiative near the home underscores the project's dedication to regenerative processes.

The property itself features a landscaped garden with native cacti and dramatic trees, each botanical species selected to strengthen the connection between the built environment and its context. The project exemplifies the power of architecture to enrich human experience by blending the boundaries between built spaces and their interaction with nature.

*Page 289*: On the coast of Oaxaca, Casa Altanera merges brutalist forms with traditional Mexican construction methods. The house is composed of three buildings: two geometric concrete structures and a thatched-roof pavilion. A folding facade of retractable timber doors opens to a native garden, creating a fluid transition between indoor and outdoor spaces.

*Preceding pages*: The open-air living pavilion sits beneath a traditional palm-thatched roof, opening on all sides to the surrounding landscape. Positioned to frame views of the ocean and hills, the living room features custom furnishings made from local timber, blending contemporary design with regional craft.

*Opposite*: Brightly colored Acapulco chairs introduce a subtle contrast to the natural tones of the surrounding greenery. The deck extends the living space outward, offering connection to the landscape.

*Preceding pages*: The bedroom opens to a private terrace, designed as a space for rest and reflection. Rigid lines are softened with timber screens, natural floors, and warm, tactile furnishings. The space feels grounded, while remaining open to the elements.

*Opposite*: The open kitchen is defined by a cast-concrete counter and a direct connection to the adjacent dining and living areas. Timber slats screen the boundary between inside and out, offering glimpses of vegetation and the Pacific beyond.

## Villa Cava / Espacio 18 Arquitectura

Standing proud, this fortress-like dwelling draws inspiration from Tetris, Mayan ruins, and the enigmatic art of M.C. Escher, creating a blend of strength and whimsy.

Villa Cava, an innovative residence in Tulum, embraces the ruggedness of brutalist architecture while harmonizing with the lush Mayan jungle surrounding it. Conceived by Oaxaca-based architecture studio Espacio 18 Arquitectura for young Canadian homeowners Adrian and Andrea, the design was informed by cenotes—ancient, water-filled limestone sinkholes common in Mexico's Yucatán Peninsula. These unique geological formations serve as the inspiration for the home's distinctive architectural design elements, infusing it with the essence and spatial qualities of the region.

Referencing these cenotes, the architects integrated water features into the robust concrete edifice. The house is crowned with a circular skylight, and this oculus serves as the base of the rooftop swimming pool, casting reflections throughout the day on the neutral surfaces in the foyer and introducing natural light into the space. This feature encourages viewers to gaze upward, as if peering out of a cenote, the blue-hued light enhancing the cavernous space and the passage of shadows acting as a kind of sundial.

Raw wood-formed concrete, chosen for its durability and low maintenance, responds adeptly to Tulum's humid climate and the threat of hurricanes. This material underpins the villa's brutalist aesthetic and functional design. Sustainability is key to the project, with passive cooling techniques employed and the preservation of existing trees informing the arrangement of pools and patios.

Architectural ingenuity continues outside, where a half-arc carport serves as a sculptural element that shields against the sun and rain. The home, as described by its creators, architects Mario Avila and Carla Osorio, is a "habitable sculpture." According to them, crafting the villa was analogous to carving stone, space-by-space, until it evolved into the occupiable sculpture that they had envisioned.

The entryway, a geometric double-height structure flanked by preserved trees that leads to a floating staircase, further emphasizes the theme of organic integration. Inside, the interiors are a conversation between the cool austerity of concrete and the warm tones of maple wood, particularly evident in the open-plan kitchen and other living spaces. These areas are designed around the central swimming pool, enhancing the sense of openness and flow. On the upper floor, rooms benefit from lofty almost thirty-foot ceilings and carefully placed skylights that invite an abundance of natural light, softening the interior spaces.

Designer Kayla Pongrác has complemented the architectural elements with a palette of light timber and neutral-toned furnishings, while the smooth concrete floors and walls mirror the exterior's brutalist aesthetic. The rooftop terrace offers an additional gathering place, furnished for relaxation and providing panoramic views of the enveloping jungle through a circular opening reminiscent of the work of Carlo Scarpa.

With its geometric contours, the concrete shelter is a demonstration of architectural creativity and respect for its spectacular natural setting—a sanctuary that plays with light, space, and material to create a unique living experience. At Villa Cava, the sum of its parts coalesces into a complete and inviting whole, showcasing a masterful blend of natural inspiration and architectural innovation.

*Page 299*: Villa Cava is a habitable sculpture by Espacio 18 Arquitectura. The half-arc carport doubles as a dramatic sculptural element shielding against rain and sun, while a rooftop pool is seamlessly embedded into the concrete structure.

*Preceding pages, left*: A skylight in the ceiling, inspired by the cenotes of the Yucatán Peninsula—ancient, water-filled limestone caves—draws natural light into the entry foyer, creating a quiet moment upon arrival.

*Preceding pages, right*: Linear planes and shifting shadows animate the concrete surfaces in a tranquil sitting area near the rooftop pool.

*Right*: A circular opening punctuates the concrete wall, demarcating the rooftop's outdoor kitchen, bar, and living space. A nod to Carlo Scarpa's work, the dramatic aperture brings sculptural clarity to this peaceful, elevated living area.

*Left*: Floor-to-ceiling glass doors erase boundaries between inside and out in the central dining and living space. Pale timber and neutral-toned furnishings soften the brutalist qualities of smooth concrete floors and walls.

## Casa Cons / Bosco Sodi

Casa Cons is not merely a retreat—it represents a deep-seated, lifelong bond with this remote expanse of coastline. On a wild stretch of Mexico's Pacific shoreline emerges Casa Cons, the seaside sanctuary of contemporary Mexican artist Bosco Sodi and his family. The haven is a testament to the artist's vision and the dialogue between nature and architecture.

Conceptualized by Sodi in collaboration with architect Samantha Redfern, the beachfront home marries raw concrete, locally sourced fired-clay bricks, and indigenous tropical timber into a series of open-air pavilions seamlessly integrated into the dense vegetation of the sandy shore. Although Sodi is not a trained architect, his personal journey with materials has resulted in a design that resonates with the architectural heritage of the region.

Sodi's creative sanctuary extends beyond this personal retreat to Casa Wabi, an artist residency and nonprofit arts foundation he established in 2014. Casa Wabi is a popular destination for design enthusiasts, featuring work by some of the world's most esteemed architects. Tadao Ando's signature cast-concrete walls form the main structure, while Álvaro Siza's ceramics studio, with its distinctive curved brick partition, centers around an imposing kiln by Alberto Kalach. Kengo Kuma's contribution is a sculptural chicken coop constructed from interlocking wooden boards, showcasing the fusion of artistry and functionality.

Taking inspiration from these architectural luminaries, Sodi crafted a home near Casa Wabi that pays homage to a rich assortment of traditional materials. Expansive concrete openings frame unobstructed ocean views, while walls of concrete and clay show the craftsmanship of local artisans. The inclined concrete roof, angled toward the ocean, not only frames the horizon and swimming pool but also facilitates natural ventilation, taking advantage of breezes from the ocean and mountainside.

This design celebrates indoor / outdoor living, seamlessly integrating the existing vegetation into its layout. Meandering paths wind through the dry tropical foliage, linking private retreats at the rear with communal beachside areas, offering an immersive engagement with nature. For decades, this coastal enclave has served as a second home for Sodi, who first camped here as a teenager and later shared this untouched stretch of coastline with his wife, Lucia Corredor, co-founder of Mexico City's design emporium, Decada. Corredor curated the beach house interiors with wooden furnishings that resonate with the rustic charm of the setting. It is an amalgam of casual and cosmopolitan; a timber Ping-Pong table and locally sourced stones set into custom clay niches, for example, harmoniously blend the natural surroundings with contemporary design.

The use of clay bricks is a nod to the traditional building practices of Oaxaca. Handmade in nearby villages, these bricks are crafted from the same clay that Sodi employs in his celebrated sculptures. In his artistic practice, Sodi engages in a tactile, intuitive process, creating canvases rich with a dense mixture of pigment, wood, glue, and natural fibers. As these materials dry, they form unique textures that crack under environmental influences, each piece distinctly revealing its context.

Much like Bosco Sodi's art does, Casa Cons pays reverence to the beauty that time unveils, embodying Sodi's concept of working in accord with the elements. Describing his artistic process, he says, "things become beautiful, the more time passes. I want to work with the elements, not against them," and these thoughts are clearly evident in his architecture.

Sharing the resilience of pre-Hispanic architecture, whose concrete edifices have withstood millennia of harsh climatic conditions, the smooth surfaces will, over time, weather beautifully, bearing the mark of salty sea air and the sea's embrace, becoming nature's canvas.

*Page 307*: Set directly on the sand, facing the Pacific Ocean, Casa Cons is the beachside retreat of Mexican artist Bosco Sodi and his family.

*Preceding pages*: Wide and low-slung, open to the elements without doors or windows, the home, designed by Sodi, embraces the sea. Its raw concrete frames the coastal terrain.

*Left*: A gently sloping roofline echoes the horizon and enables natural ventilation, allowing coastal breezes to drift through the interiors styled by designer Lucia Corredor.

*Following pages, left*: Vibrant, colorful tiles bring an unexpected burst of character to the otherwise minimalist concrete kitchen, where built-in shelves showcase Oaxacan pottery.

*Following pages, right*: Locally sourced clay bricks root the space in the region's building traditions. Stones as sculptures are arranged in clay niches.

*Pages 314–15*: A custom wood table tennis table designed by the Mexican atelier Taller Bok stands against a clay brick wall, where niches hold a curated collection of rocks.

*Page 316*: At the entrance, a terra-cotta clay wall encourages cross-ventilation. A wooden chair, clay vessel, and driftwood piece set the tone—organic, elemental.

*Page 317*: A rustic wooden bench placed beneath a row of sun hats. Just as Sodi's art embraces elemental forces, Casa Cons celebrates time's passage—beauty found in weathered textures, patinas, and simplicity.

## Casa Aviv / CO-LAB Design Office

Brutalism meets nature in Casa Aviv, a modern residence embodying minimalist rigor and artisanal allure, nestled in the jungle of Tulum. Designed by CO-LAB Design Office, led by Joana Gomes and Joshua Beck, this serene haven's austere restraint is the result of architectural sophistication and a desire for sustainability.

Casa Aviv's architectural narrative transcends boundaries, blending indoor and outdoor spaces as a unified whole. CO-LAB's design philosophy embraces nature's profound impact on human experiences, treating landscapes and gardens as integral elements of spatial composition. This fusion creates an immersive sanctuary where the line between interior and exterior fades away, enveloping occupants in a tranquil environment.

The residence comprises two elongated structures, with floor-to-ceiling pivot glass doors in the living and dining areas that open up completely to the pool and verdant jungle garden, maximizing cross ventilation.

Embracing global design philosophies, especially Japanese *wabi-sabi*, the designers celebrate imperfection and organic beauty. This ethos is evident in the use of *shou sugi ban* on local hardwoods; this ancient Japanese technique seals and strengthens wood by charring it. Handmade finishes by skilled local artisans add distinctive character, showing the importance of human touch and cultural heritage in construction.

Casa Aviv pays homage to Mexico's rich cultural heritage through its use of traditional craftsmanship and locally-sourced materials. This selection of simple materials reflects a commitment to sustainability and resilience in the face of Tulum's hot, humid climate. Further connecting the house to its locale, warm, earth-toned concrete walls counterbalance black marble terrazzo floors.

The austere interiors are sparsely furnished with handcrafted furniture, lighting, and textiles designed by CO-LAB, imparting artisanal authenticity and cultural richness to the seaside sanctuary. Casa Aviv, a dialogue between architecture and nature, offers a nurturing living experience that reflects the beauty of its tropical location while revering timeless principles of design and sustainability.

*Page 319*: Monumental floor-to-ceiling pivoting glass doors in the double-height living and dining areas of Casa Aviv open fully to the pool and jungle garden beyond, inviting cross-ventilation and dissolving boundaries between indoors and out.

*Preceding pages*: Interior and exterior spaces merge seamlessly, unified by material and light. A stone wall anchors the view, while lush greenery becomes an essential element of the architectural language. CO-LAB's vision integrates nature into every gesture.

*Opposite*: Wooden furniture sits in dialogue with the surrounding jungle. On the table, resin vessels by Mexican designer Mónica Calderón add an artisanal touch.

*Following pages, left*: The living space opens toward the garden and pool, designed to invite rest and calm. Rich wooden tones balance the vibrant greens of the jungle. The table, benches, and sofa were designed by CO-LAB and handcrafted by local artisans.

*Following pages, right*: Kitchen cabinetry is crafted from locally sourced hardwood and finished in *shou sugi ban*, a traditional Japanese technique that preserves wood through charring—combining strength, simplicity, and depth of texture.

## La Extraviada / EM Estudio

Perched above the tranquil coastal community of Mazunte, Oaxaca, La Extraviada honors its seaside surroundings. Conceived by EM Estudio's Ivan Esqueda Martínez and interior designer Gala Sánchez-Renero as their personal haven, this holiday home melds effortlessly into a forest reserve, overlooking the scenic Mermejita beach and the southernmost tip of Mexico, Punta Cometa.

La Extraviada provides a profound connection with the ocean and the mountain, presenting itself as an organic extension of the landscape.

Site-specific, the design is comprised of cubic forms following the mountain's contours and evokes a feeling of stacked stones poised on the hillside. Pathways interweave among the structures, which descend toward the sea, creating an unfolding journey through the property's various elevations and spaces. The architecture is a narrative of exploration, where each step reveals a new aspect of this home, embedded within its verdant natural surroundings.

Concrete serves as the primary material in La Extraviada's construction, and surfaces finished with a rich, brown-pigmented polished cement blend seamlessly with the environment. This is further enhanced by the use of locally sourced timber and stone, and the inclusion of black, blue, and green cement tiles echo the volcanic black sands, the azure sea, and the verdant forest hues, encapsulating the essence of the coastal environment.

The architectural philosophy of EM Estudio revolves around a symbiotic relationship with nature. Rather than imposing upon the landscape, the design of La Extraviada embraces and harnesses the elements—sunlight, airflow, and humidity—and transforms potential obstacles into beneficial features that enhance the dwelling. Open pavilions, designed for optimal airflow, adapt seamlessly to varying needs for light, ventilation, or privacy. Martínez's design fosters a profound connection with the outdoors, where the nearby ocean is a soothing and constant companion.

La Extraviada celebrates the synergy between architecture and nature. Its name, referencing a folktale about a fish that inspired a dream and ultimately, a home, symbolizes more than a personal sanctuary; it is proof of Martínez and Sánchez-Renero's artistic vision and collaborative spirit. The dwelling is not only integrated with its vibrant coastal setting but also elevates it, becoming an enduring part of the natural canvas. La Extraviada transcends mere structure; its forms inserted in the landscape are destined to blend with and enhance the natural beauty that envelops it.

*Preceding page*: At the southernmost tip of Mexico, La Extraviada unfolds as an organic extension of the land. Staggered structures descend the densely vegetated hillside, embracing the Pacific Ocean in a silent dialogue with nature.

*Right*: The ocean is a constant, soothing presence. Conceived by architect Ivan Esqueda Martínez and interior designer Gala Sánchez-Renero of EM Estudio as their personal retreat, the residence reflects a deep connection to place.

*Following pages, left*: Concrete forms the house's architectural backbone. In the kitchen, surfaces are finished in polished concrete pigmented with rich earth tones and black tiles, echoing the terrain and nearby volcanic sand beaches.

*Following pages, right*: Accents of black, green, and blue concrete tiles evoke the surrounding elements: the volcanic sands, the forest canopy, and the sea. Together, they anchor the home in its coastal context.

*Opposite*: The spaces are designed to adapt—offering shade, light, seclusion, or breeze. The architecture is flexible, responding to the rhythm of the environment.

*Right*: A home for rest and inspiration. Each space holds its own mood and purpose. The house opens fully to welcome sun and air, yet can close to offer protection, intimacy, and stillness.

## Casa Shalva / Arquitectura Mixta & Aviv Siso

This brutalist hacienda, immersed in Tulum's jungle, embraces the craftsmanship of Mexican artisans and the lushness it is surrounded by.

Casa Shalva is anything but standard, with its nods to ancient Mayan temples and views of the lush Tulum tropical jungle. The numerous curves and arches amidst the formidable angles of cement lend a delicate, airy feel to the structure, helped also by oversized windows throughout.

The brutalist style extols raw base materials—cement and stone—and highlights a distinct monochrome palette seen within the house's hues of grays, and use of steel, glass, and timber. Despite the dwelling's feeling of solidity, the mood is gentle and serene—qualities established when stepping across the threshold and into its calm atmosphere.

The homeowner, Belgian-Israeli entrepreneur and property developer Aviv Siso, explains that in Hebrew the word *shalva* suggests the sensation of peace and serenity. With the design of Casa Shalva, he has merged his love of nature, abundant space, minimalism, and clean lines.

Born in Antwerp and raised in Israel, Siso eventually moved to New York and then to Tulum. His Belgian origins informed the retreat's aesthetic, especially the concept of finding beauty in humility and understatement. Here, beauty is found in simplicity and in constant discovery. It is found in spaces with great appreciation for details, in grand open spaces, and in the quality materials used throughout.

Collaborating on the design with local firm Arquitectura Mixta, Siso completed his very personal holiday home with the help of designer Alexandra Pedregal, with design and stone furnishings by Sublime Studios. Plans merged modern architecture with the feel of a Mexican hacienda. The aim was to create a space that nurtured a feeling of calm with an open, flowing floor plan with neutral tones, combining natural stone from the area, warm timber, and polished cement, employing skilled Mexican artisans.

A profusion of tropical plants and sensitive landscaping allows the house to blend into the surrounding jungle. Siso has a profound respect and appreciation for masterful craftsmanship. "The beautiful polished concrete and the cement and stonework are entrenched in Mexican building culture and tradition. The tone of the cement color—gray and masculine—contrasts beautifully with the greenery."

A series of archways softening the austere brutalist structure are reminiscent of both a modern-day hacienda and a traditional Moroccan riad. There are common rooms set around the courtyard's central pool, and the overall layout offers a sense of discovery from different perspectives and vantage points.

Sculptural raw stone furnishings, whose materiality and forms are in perfect alignment with the architecture, utilize local Crema Maya limestone. "Its neutral base and veining adds a sense of natural movement to the material that creates a feeling of nature within the sculpted pieces," says Sublime Studios founder and designer Stephanie Ström, who credits sculptor Constantin Brancusi as inspiration.

Unique and beautiful pieces of functional art, the massive dining table, benches, and chairs of rawly hewn limestone dominate the open kitchen, dining, and entertainment area. Below is a sunken living area with a built-in sectional sofa and a stone firepit coffee table.

Upstairs, secluded bedrooms overlook treetops, an outdoor rooftop bar offers sunset views, and a plunge pool on the uppermost balcony permits stargazing. As Siso summarizes, "this is a house that ultimately needs to be enjoyed with an ensemble of wonderful humans and creatives—to give space to express and share art, music, meditation, food, and create memories."

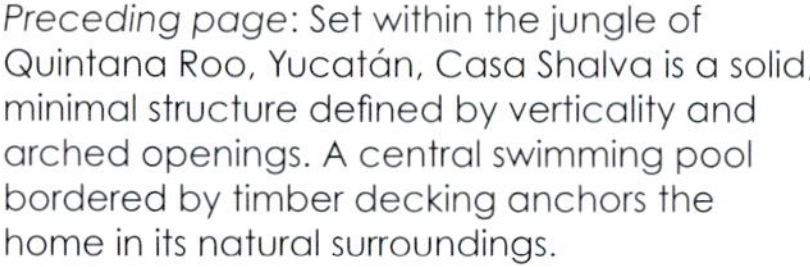

*Preceding page*: Set within the jungle of Quintana Roo, Yucatán, Casa Shalva is a solid, minimal structure defined by verticality and arched openings. A central swimming pool bordered by timber decking anchors the home in its natural surroundings.

*Right*: A sequence of arches softens the geometry of the structure, evoking the layout of a modern-day hacienda. Rooms and halls unfold around the courtyard pool. A monumental rough-hewn limestone dining table with matching benches, custom designed by Sublime Studios, underscores the enduring role of stone in Mexican design tradition.

*Left*: The surrounding jungle is a natural backdrop to the sunken living area. At its center, a sculptural firepit coffee table by Sublime Studios, crafted from local Crema Maya limestone, anchors the space with elemental simplicity.

*Right*: Natural materials—warm timber, stone, and a woven Mexican rug—lend softness and warmth to the poolside bedroom. Large windows open to lush greenery, inviting the outdoors in.

*Opposite*: A handwoven Yucatán hammock is paired with sculptural chairs by Sublime Studios. "These are all about functioning form, materiality, and art," says founder Stephanie Ström. "The chairs are sculptures—meant to be used, or simply admired."

## Acknowledgments

Richard Powers and I extend our heartfelt thanks to all the architects, designers, artists, and creatives who welcomed us into their homes, shared their projects, and opened their studios, allowing us the privilege and opportunity to capture the unique essence and spirit of their work. With much gratitude, we thank the following individuals—in no particular order: Manuel Cervantes, Emmanuel Picault / Chic by Accident, Marcos Ruiz, Héctor Barroso THB, Carla Fernández & Pedro Reyes, Alberto Kalach / TAX, Bosco Sodi, Lucia Corredor, Graciela Iturbide, Manuel Rocha Diaz & Gabriela Carrillo, Ludwig Godefroy, Sergio Escamilla, Javier Sanchez JSa Arquitectura & Robert Hutchison RHA, Alfonso Quiñones / BAAQ, Claudio Sodi, Carlos H. Matos, Aranza de Ariño, Karla Lisker, Alberto Calleja TAC, Alonso de Garay ADG, Micaela de Bernardí MDB, Valérie Boerma & Bart van Seggelen / Barde vanVoltt, Gala Sánchez-Renero & Ivan Esqueda Martínez / EM Estudio MX, Estudio IZA Arquitectura, Mónica Calderón & Ezequiel Farca, Aviv Siso, Joana Gomes & Joshua Beck / CO-LAB Design Office, Arquitectura Mixta, Sublime Studios, Mario Avila & Carla Osorio / Espacio 18 Arquitectura, Adrian Salamunovic & Andrea Fox, Rogelio Vallejo Bores, Oscar Didier Ascencio Castro, Nik Zaret / HW Studio, and Kurimanzutto gallerists Mónica Manzutto & José Kuri.

Immense thanks to Javier Senosiain, the Barragán family, Barragan Foundation, the Egerstrom family, Ricardo Legorreta, and the Hernández Navarro family.

In memory of Agustín Hernández Navarro, who, just weeks before his passing at the age of ninety-eight, showed us grace, enthusiasm, and kindness as he helped organize the photographing of his iconic project Praxis. Much gratitude to Roberto Hernández.

We offer our sincere appreciation to the following individuals for their contributions: Steffi Ström, Michael Gleeson, Carla Sodi, Juliette Frey, Lena Norling, The Traveling Beetle, Sophie MDB, Raquel Canales.

We'd like to express gratitude to the incredible team at Rizzoli for helping to bring this book to life and supporting our vision. Special thanks to editor Douglas Curran for getting us started, to senior editor and designer Daniel Melamud for taking on the project and for turning it into this beautiful tome, and to publisher Charles Miers for believing in our work from the beginning. What began as a passion project evolved into a journey—drawn to the rich history, architecture, design, and craftsmanship of Mexico, we were continually inspired by the extraordinary talent behind these remarkable creations. Along the way, we were rewarded with unforgettable experiences, new friendships, and the discovery of incredible landscapes, buildings, and artists.

*Nuestro más sincero agradecimiento a todos los que formaron parte de este proyecto* (Our deepest thanks to all who were part of this project).

Lastly, with love and gratitude, I dedicate this book to my son Luca Carballo Christiansen, for your adventurous spirit as a fellow traveler with me on this journey during our long stay throughout the making of this book. You are part of this story (see page 300) and part of mine. *Gracias, besitos mi amor!*

First published in the United States of America in 2026
by Rizzoli International Publications, Inc.
49 West 27th Street
New York, NY 10001
www.rizzoliusa.com


Foreword by Eugenio López Alonso
Text and styling by Tami Christiansen
Photography by Richard Powers



Edited and designed by Daniel Melamud
Publisher: Charles Miers
Production Director: Maria Pia Gramaglia
Copyeditor: Victoria Brown

ISBN: 978-0-8478-7639-6
Library of Congress Control Number: 2025944586

Printed in China
2026 2027 2028 2029 / 10 9 8 7 6 5 4 3 2 1

The authorized representative in the EU for product safety and compliance is Mondadori Libri S.p.A. via Gian Battista Vico 42, Milan, Italy, 20123
www.mondadori.it

Visit us online:
Instagram.com/RizzoliBooks
Facebook.com/RizzoliNewYork
Youtube.com/user/RizzoliNY